Slovakia Travel for Tourism

History, Tour, Culture, People and Environment

Author
Fisayo Lowe

Copyright Notice

Copyright © 2017 Global Print Digital
All Rights Reserved

<u>Digital Management Copyright Notice</u>. This Title is not in public domain, it is copyrighted to the original author, and being published by **Global Print Digital**. No other means of reproducing this title is accepted, and none of its content is editable, neither right to commercialize it is accepted, except with the consent of the author or authorized distributor. You must purchase this Title from a vendor who's right is given to sell it, other sources of purchase are not accepted, and accountable for an action against. We are happy that you understood, and being guided by these terms as you proceed. Thank you

First Printing: 2017.

ISBN: 978-1-912483-57-0

Publisher: Global Print Digital.
Arlington Row, Bibury, Cirencester GL7 5ND
Gloucester
United Kingdom.
Website: www.homeworkoffer.com
.

CONTENT

Introduction 1
History 3
   The Territory of Slovakia before the Arrival of the Slavs 3
   The Arrival of the Slavs and Construction of a State 6
   Slovakia as a part of the Hungarian Kingdom 8
   Century of Change 11
   The Anjou Period 13
   The Late Middle Ages 15
   Between Two Civilisations 17
   The Road to National Emancipation 25
   In State Political Transformation until 1918 31
   Slovakia in the Czechoslovak Republic 40
   Slovakia During the Second World War: 1939–1945 50
   After the War (1945–1948). 41 Years of Communist Totality (1948–1989) 55
   In the Democratic World 71
Government 78
   Education system 79
   Health & safety 81
Economy 83
People and Culture 85
   The Culture, Traditions, and Heritage 85
   Religion 87
   Languages 88
   Gastronomy 89
Travel and Tourism 91
   Travel Guide 91
   Things to Do 94
   Attractions 97
   Holidays and Festivals 101
   Food and Restaurants 105
   Shopping and Leisure 108

Transportation *110*

Airports *112*

Travel Tips *114*

Locations *116*

Regions and things to do... *117*

    Bratislava 117

    Trencin 120

    Banska 122

    Presov 123

    Trnava 125

    Nitra 127

    Zilina 129

    Kosice 130

Tourist Regions *132*

    Liptov 132

        Demänovská Cave of Liberty 133

        Demänovská Ice Cave 135

        Vlkolínec 137

        Museum of Liptov village in Pribylina 138

        Prosiecka and Kvacianska valley 140

        Havránok - Celtic settlement 141

        Skipark Jasna Nizke Tatry.. 142

        Stanisovska Cave.. 144

        Vazecka Cave 145

    Orava 146

        Orava Castle 146

        Oravska priehrada (Orava Dam) 149

        SKI Oravice 150

    Spiš 151

    Spis Castle 151

    Dobšinská Ice Cave 153

    Ski Mlynky 154

visas 157

    Health and Safety 158

Climate 159

Introduction

Slovakia's humble tourism motto, "A Part of Europe Worth Visiting," seems to sum up the country's rather modest ambitions when it comes to luring visitors. Just barely a teenager Slovakia became an independent nation in 1993 the country still seems unsure of itself and what it has to offer. But the motto surely underestimates Slovakia's very winning charms. The mountains, starting in the hills of the Malá Fatra and running east to the Alpine peaks of the High Tatras, are some of the most starkly beautiful in Europe. And it's unlikely that any country in Europe, or anywhere else for that matter, has a castle with the pure drop-dead shock value of Spisský Hrad.

Slovakia's youthful capital, Bratislava, has shed some of its hulking Communist-era architecture and fixed up its charming Old Town. The result is a fun, lively, and energetic city that makes Vienna feel fusty and overly mannered and Prague feel forced and overly touristed by comparison. And the Slovaks' humility is part of the charm. The rudeness or arrogance you sometimes find in more popular destinations is absent here. Just let slip in conversation that you've come all the way from the United States, or Canada, or wherever, and the reaction you get will be nothing short of amazement. You'll feel like a treasured guest.

To be sure, you may have to put up with some relative hardships now and then. Standards for food and lodging, especially off the beaten track, are a slight step down from western Europe, and even perhaps lower than you might find in the Czech Republic or Hungary. But don't let that deter you. Relax, enjoy the largely unspoiled countryside, take a meal and a glass of wine in a traditional *koliba* restaurant, and let the natural warmth and hospitality of the people win you over.

History

The Territory of Slovakia before the Arrival of the Slavs

With an area of more than 49 thousand km sq., Slovakia extends between the River Morava to the west and River Tisza to the east, the middle Danube to the south and Tatra mountains to the north. Humans have lived on this territory since the late Stone Age. So-called Neanderthal man has been discovered at the sites of the oldest settlements from the Middle Palaeolithic period in Gánovce near Poprad and Šaľa on the Váh. Nomadic settlements of mammoth hunters appeared here in the Upper Palaeolithic period. The best works of European prehistoric art include the Venus of Moravany, which was found to be 22,800 years old.

During the Neolithic period there was a substantial change in prehistoric man's way of life, which is usually characterised as the Neolithic revolution. In the 6th and 5th millennia BC, the farmers of the new Neolithic civilisation, who had begun to cultivate crops and domesticate animals in addition to hunting, started to move to the Danube basin. The people of the Lengyel culture built a number of settlements with dozens of houses in south-western Slovakia in the Middle Neolithic period. These settlements often also included earth fortifications (rondelas) as centres of local administration.

The territory of Slovakia became a part of advanced European civilisation in the Bronze Age (1900–700 BC) due to trade. The rich deposits of copper ore in the central Slovak area enabled bronze implements, jewellery and weapons to be made. Important centres of trade and power were established in this period. These consisted of stone houses arranged into regular streets laid with stone cobbles (settlement in Spišský štvrtok) and in south-western Slovakia the local centre in Nitriansky Hrádok had a similar status. These centres died out after 1500 BC under the influence of the Mediterranean Minoan and Mycenaean civilisations.

Significant cultural and demographic progress was made on the territory of Slovakia in the Iron Age. Celts made their way here from their original homes around AD 400. These Celt warriors built large reinforced towns (*oppida*) in south-western Slovakia. There was even a Celt mint in the Bratislava *oppidum*.

In the last decades BC, the Romans conquered Pannonia and started to build a system of fortresses on the river Danube (*Limes Romanus*). The Germanic Quadi and Marcomanni tribes settled north of the Danube. Periods of peaceful co-existence were broken by periods when the Germans attempted to infiltrate the rich Roman provinces. The Romans perfected their system of defence on the Danube in the 2nd century and started to move their fortresses to the Danube's northern bank (Devín, Bratislava, Iža near Komárno). Germanic society, mainly its ruling class, was greatly influenced by Roman civilisation. The Germanic nobility promoted trade with the Roman provinces in times of peace.

Relations between the Romans and Germans broke down under the reign of Marcus Aurelius (161–180), when Roman legions managed to gain supremacy after several campaigns and penetrated far north into enemy territory. The Roman inscription in Trenčín from 179 is proof of this. The Romanisation of the Barbarian population continued in the late Roman period (181–380). Many Roman buildings appeared on the territory of south-western Slovakia (Bratislava-Dúbravka, Cífer-Pác, Veľký Kýr) in the relatively peaceful period of the 3rd and 4th centuries. These were probably residences of the pro-Roman Quadi aristocracy.

There was a significant ethnic shift in Europe following the fall of the Roman Empire. The Carpathian basin's fate was greatly influenced by the invasion of the Huns in 375, who quickly built up a powerful Hun empire. A defeat in Catalonia in 451 halted its expansion westwards. The conquered tribes took advantage of the feared Attila's death to destroy the Huns' empire.

The Arrival of the Slavs and Construction of a State

The first Slav tribes began to settle in the Middle Danube area near the end of the 5th century. They met with the remaining Germanic population on their conquered territories and the ethnic substrate of the Púchov and later Przeworski cultures in the mountain valleys. The Slav farmers mainly sought out lowland regions with quality soil, rich pasture and sufficient water. They also brought knowledge of how to find, extract and manipulate iron ore from their original homeland. Handmade Prague type ceramics are also typical of the ancient Slavs. They lived in small settlements consisting of several single room huts built into the ground. They cremated their dead on the outskirts.

The nomadic Avars led by Khagab Bajan became the hegemony of the Carpathian basin in 568. Thanks to their excellent weapons and nomadic military tactics, they quickly conquered the Slavs, moving to the Danube's northern bank and taking the lowland area of southern Slovakia at the end of the 6th century. They took advantage of the population's economic potential and were often violent towards them. This provoked a large anti-Avar rebellion around 620. In 623, the rebels chose the Frankish merchant Samo as their king, and he successfully warded off all the Avars' attempts to regain supremacy.

The core of Samo's empire extended along the Danube. Besides what is now Slovakia, it also included Moravia and a part of Austria and Bohemia. The strength of Samo's empire was also shown by the conflict with the Frankish king Dagobert in 631. Samo's Slavs completely overwhelmed the Frankish forces under the Vogastisburg castle. King Samo died in 658 and his empire was split into smaller units. The Avars used this to partially renew their hegemony in this area.

Slav principalities started to form along the edge of the Carpathian basin in the 8th century. The Nitra principality formed along the Danube and the Morava principality in southern Moravia. The principality took advantage of Charlemagne's defeat of the Avars and, with the help of armed forces, crushed the remains of Avar power and seized their settlements. The forefathers of prince Pribina built a walled town in Nitra lying in the middle of an important agglomeration of settlements.

After destroying the Avars' power, they started to expand into their neighbours' territories. In the early 9th century, the Principality of Nitra's power had already spread north to the Small and White Carpathians, south to the Danube and east as far as the Spiš region. The prince secured the conquered territories by building fortified towns. The process of the Danube Slavs' conversion to Christianity started in the 820s. Prince Pribina demonstrated an inclination towards Christianity when he took a Christian from Bavaria as his bride and had a Christian church built at his seat in Nitra, which the Archbishop of Salzburg Adalram consecrated in 828.

Slovakia as a part of the Hungarian Kingdom

After the Magyars' victory in a battle with the Bavarians near Bratislava in 907, the union of Magyar tribes became the military hegemony in the Carpathian basin. Following the fall of Great Moravia, the territory of Slovakia had split into smaller units led by members of the local aristocracy. Many of them used the changed conditions to join the Magyars and participate in their raids on western Europe. These raids ended in 955 with the Magyars' catastrophic defeat on the river Lech. The Magyars were forced to adopt a settled way of life while taking advantage of the resident Slav population.

They laid the foundations of the Hungarian state in the second half of the 10th century under the leadership of the Árpád dynasty, and prince Géza adopted Christianity. The territory of Slovakia did not lose its importance and the principality of Nitra became the seat of Géza's younger brother Michael. Géza removed Michael in 995 and replaced him with his son Stephen, who married the Bavarian princess Gisela and became a fervent missionary. He succeeded his father Géza as prince in 997. However, another member of the Árpád line, Koppany, opposed Stephen and challenged his claim. In a decisive moment the Slovak magnates Hunt, Poznan and Orzius helped Stephen and defeated Koppany with their combined forces. With this, they gained a significant influence over Stephen and became his closest confidants.

The ethnogenesis of Slovaks was not disrupted in the conditions of the 10th century. In the new situation, they became the largest ethnic group in the Carpathian basin. They preserved their language, specific culture, awareness of solidarity and Nitra remained their natural centre.

Stephen was crowned the first Hungarian king in 1000 and Hungary became an independent church province. Shortly after Stephen's coronation the Polish king Boleslaw the Great overpowered the territory of Slovakia and entrusted it to the administration of Michael's son Ladislas. This lasted even after Boleslaw's death, until 1029, when Stephen I took advantage of the Poles' weakening influence and took Slovakia for himself. He threw the younger brother of Ladislas Lysy Vazul into prison and entrusted the administration of the Nitra principality to his son Emmerich. Vazul's sons Andrew, Béla and Levente fled abroad in the face of possible reprisals. It is their descendants that became the Árpád kings.

The great pagan uprising of 1046 brought Andrew I, who had until then been held in Kiev, to the throne. He called his younger brother Béla from Poland and appointed him to administer the so-called third kingdom, consisting of Nitra (11 *comitates*) and Bihar (4 *comitates*). He had his own army, conducted foreign policy relatively independently and even minted his own coins. When Bela eventually became king, Nitra fell to his sons Géza, Ladislas and Lampert. These had to compete with their cousin king Solomon. They finally defeated him with Czech help in a battle near Mogyoród in 1074. Military squads of Nitrans were also honoured in this battle.

King Ladislas I (1077–1095), who saw to the beatification of the first Hungarian saints, was succeeded by his nephew Coloman. The Nitra principality fell to his younger brother Álmos. Álmos was not content with his status and took up arms against his brother a number of times. In 1108 king Coloman lost his patience, blinded Álmos and abolished the Nitra principality. Coloman partially redressed his decision by establishing an episcopacy in Nitra.

The settlement of Slovakia was gradually completed during the 12th century. The whole country was divided into royal *comitates* headed by *župans* appointed by the king. These secured the collection of taxes and dues in kind from the population, judged all disputes and led the *comitatus'* army. A wide network of serving settlements and royal courts secured the needs of the ruling classes of Hungarian society.

Century of Change

The prevailing royal possession of land rapidly started to come to an end in the early 13th century and the Hungarian nobility's power and status grew quickly. This process most threatened lesser royal servants, who forced king Andrew II to issue a so-called Golden Bull in 1222. This formulated the rights and obligations of the king and nobility in written form for the first time. In the first years of his reign, king Béla IV (1235–1270) realised that the break-up of royal patrimonial property could not be halted. Therefore he decided to gain new support in the privileged medieval towns which started to appear on the territory of Slovakia even before the Tartar invasion.

The oldest included Trnava, Banská Štiavnica, Krupina, Zvolen, and Bratislava. Privileges were granted which gave rise to self-governing communities led by town councils elected by burghers. The burghers had the right to manage their property without restriction and could move freely. These granted privileges enabled the burghers to perform various economic activities, mainly trade and crafts. The towns had to pay an agreed amount to the royal treasury and send a certain number of armed men to the royal army for their privileged status.

This promising process of establishing towns was halted by the unexpected invasion of the Tartars in 1241/1242. On 11th April 1241 they defeated the royal army near the river Slaná and then ravaged the whole country for more than a year. The territory of Slovakia, especially its mountainous areas, was mostly spared. Well fortified towns and castles (Trenčín, Bratislava, Nitra, Komárno, Fiľakovo) also resisted the Tartars. In the summer of 1242, the Tartar forces unexpectedly pulled back. After his restoration, king Béla IV decided to invite foreign settlers, who came here mainly from the German lands, to the depopulated areas. The Germans settled in both the newly forming towns and rural settlements.

Under the reign of the last kings of the House of Árpád Ladislas IV (1272–1290) and Andrew III (1290–1301) the Hungarian nobility's power grew exceptionally. Particularly during Ladislas IV's youth, members of the most powerful noble families started to build large domains with stone castles. Of these, the Csák line gained a dominant position on the territory of western Slovakia and Omodeus from the Amadei line in eastern Slovakia. The noble oligarchs stopped respecting the royal power. Matthew Csák of Trenčín created his own dominion, which consisted of 50 castles. At his seat in Trenčín he behaved like a small king and commanded his own army.

The Anjou Period

The disruption in the country was only halted by Charles Robert of Anjou, who defeated the Amadei forces in a battle near Košice in 1312 and also took over Matthew Csák's domains following his death in 1321. He renewed royal supremacy and consolidated conditions in the country through economic reforms. He introduced coin reform and started to mint gold pieces in addition to silver coins in Kremnica. Thanks to the introduction of landowners' freedom to mine, intensive mining also began on the nobility's properties.

The valley and mountain areas of central and northern Slovakia were settled on purchase or German rights, which were more advantageous for the new settlers than the older customary rights. New towns were added to the older privileged towns from the 13th century and small towns belonging to landowners (*oppida*) also appeared in individual regions as trade and industrial centres of local importance. During the 14th century, Slovakia became one of the most urbanised parts of Hungary. The German minority gained a dominant position in the majority of towns. There was a gradual Slovakisation in many towns in the second half of the 14th century and Slovaks started to sit on town councils.

There was a significant cultural development of the territory of Slovakia during the 14th century. The gothic centres of medieval towns appeared with tall local and monastery churches with rich outer and inner decoration. Artistic and architectonic monuments from this period (Levoča, Kežmarok, Košice, Bardejov, Prešov) are admired even today.

Charles Robert was succeeded by his son Louis I (1342–1382). Right at the beginning of his reign he became involved in costly battles for the Neapolitan succession. In 1351, the king rewarded the fighting nobility by issuing a law which enshrined the inalienability of the nobles' property and declared the formal equality of all members of the nobility. In 1370 after the death of his relation Kazimír I, Louis I was also named Polish king, creating the Hungarian-Polish personal union. As Louis I did not father male successors, he took pains to secure rights of succession for his daughters Hedviga and Mary towards the end of his reign.

The Late Middle Ages

After the death of Louis I, his daughter Mary and her husband Sigismund of Luxembourg (1387–1437) started to reign in Hungary. King Sigismund was not liked by the Hungarian aristocracy and he therefore tried to gain their favour with lavish donations. By the end of the 14th century he had given away two thirds of his royal castle estates. In 1401 the highest representatives of the Hungarian nobility even imprisoned the king and started to search for a more advantageous replacement. The king's trusted magnate of Polish origin Stibor of Śćiborzyc and Beckov rescued him from this difficult situation. The rebellion against King Sigismund was repeated again in 1403. With Stibor's help, the king quickly dealt with the rebels and conditions in the country stabilised. At this time, Sigismund decided to pull towns into internal policy and in 1405 issued a so-called *decretum minus* (small decree) through which town representatives gained the right to participate in sessions of the class diet. In 1408 the king reconciled with the Hungarian nobility and started to intervene very actively into European politics, especially after being named Holy Roman Emperor in 1410.

After the death of his brother Václav IV, he was also crowned king of Bohemia in 1420. But the Hussites refused to recognise him and Sigismund entered into a long struggle with them, which he never won. From 1428 the Hussites switched to an anti-offensive, organising annual military campaigns on the territory of Slovakia and also left permanent garrisons here. The situation calmed down partially after 1434, when the Hussites gradually pulled out of Slovakia.

After Sigismund, his son-in-law Albrecht Habsburg reigned for a short time. His unexpected death led to feudal anarchy and a struggle for succession. The widowed queen Elizabeth attempted to keep the crown for her underage son Ladislas Posthumous. The Hungarian Diet, however, voted for Wladislaw Jagiello (1440–1444), from whom they expected active defence of the southern borders threatened by the Ottoman Empire. Queen Elizabeth hired captain Jan Jiskra of Brandýs, who gradually occupied key locations on the territory of Slovakia at the head of an around 5 thousand strong force. The majority of his soldiers were former Hussite fighters. They often left their leader and lived by robbing the surrounding areas. They built fortified camps for defence and called themselves brethren.

The anarchy in Hungary ended after Mathias Corvinus' succession as king in 1458. The young lord soon shook off his guardians and started to build a centralised monarchy. Thanks to a tax reform, he gained the finance needed to maintain a strong army. The first university—Accademia Istropolitana—was established in Bratislava upon his initiative in 1465. At the instigation of the Roman Curia, Mathias Corvinus entered into war with the Czech king George of Podi brady and the Moravian classes named him Czech king. Towards the end of his reign, he waged war on the Austrian lands and moved his seat to Vienna.

The end of the middle ages was signified by the weak reigns of Wladislaw II Jagiello (1490–1516) and his son Louis II (1516–1526), who gradually lost control over events in the country. Neither did the unruly Hungarian classes manage to pull the country from anarchy. The Ottomans took advantage of Hungary's weakness and launched an open attack against the once powerful monarchy in 1526.

Between Two Civilisations

The Hungarian army's defeat by the Ottomans at the end of August 1526 and end of the Jagiello dynasty symbolically meant the end of the medieval Hungarian state. In the second half of the century, the territory of Slovakia became the centre of European attention and essentially the main centre of the Hungarian monarchy. Meanwhile the border of two civilisations—Christian and Muslim—was built here. The rising Habsburg dynasty integrated this part of Europe more strongly into the continent's developments. The border with the Ottoman empire, which represented another world, culture and religion, endured to the south of Slovakia for almost 150 years. The constant alternation of military conflicts with periods of peace did not create space for the more peaceful economic and social development of this region. The fact that the centre of the Hungarian monarchy also became an arena of constant armed conflicts between the Hungarian nobility and royal court, which were waged with religious, class or other battle cries, added to the disruptive momentum.

The Hungarian army's defeat and death of king Louis II at Mohacs led to fear all over Europe. Ferdinand Habsburg and Transylvanian Duke John Zapolya laid claim to the throne. Both were crowned as king and civil war broke out. The Turks used the armed conflict between the two kings to intervene militarily. The civil war ended with a peace treaty on 24.2.1538, through which both actors were recognised as legitimate rulers. In 1541 the sultan intervened in favour of John Zapolya's son John Sigismund, who was born two months after his father's death. The Turks settled Buda in August 1541, which became the centre of the new Ottoman province and base for the century and a half of attacks on the territory controlled by the Habsburgs. And so Bratislava became the capital and coronation city of the Hungarian kingdom. The Esztergom archbishop and chapter was moved to Trnava.

The defeat of Hassan the pasha in 1593 on the Croatian border was an excuse to declare war, which became known as the Fifteen Years War. Military operations took place with alternating success. In the summer of 1603, a new war was started with Persia and the Ottoman Empire was forced to find a way to conclude peace. On 11th November 1606, representatives of the fighting sides concluded the Peace of Žitava, which lasted until 1663. The conclusion of peace in 1606 did not prevent border beys from undertaking raids on the territory of Slovakia.

In March 1663, the Grand Vizier Ahmed Küprülü pushed into Hungary with his army. On 17th August 1663 the Ottomans besieged one of the most powerful anti-Turk fortresses—Nové Zámky. The defenders of Nové Zámky capitulated on 25th September 1663. Nitra, Levice and

Novohrad fell to the Turks at the same time. Nové Zámky became the centre of an Ottoman province with around 750 villages. On 1st August 1664, the Turks' advance was stopped near St. Gotthard.

Peace was signed in Vasvár soon after the battle, which confirmed the Turkish conquests. To replace Nové Zámky, a new fortress, Leopoldov, was built on the right bank of the Váh. On 31st March 1683 the Ottoman army stirred with the aim of conquering Vienna. On 12th September, after two months of besiegement, the Ottoman army defeated the allied forces. A period of liberating Hungary ensued. Charles of Lorraine defeated Nové Zámky on 19th August 1685. Less than two weeks later Buda—the centre of Ottoman power, fell. And so Slovakia finally shook off its unpleasant neighbour.

In January 1604, the Emperor's General Barbiano Belgiojoso seized protestants in the Košice cathedral. This event became a spark igniting discontent among the Protestant nobility, which armed itself and defended its privileges from this point and all through the 17th century. The discontent nobility protested and when Emperor Rudolph II ignored their complaints, Stephen Bocskay used the Protestant classes' discontent to launch an armed action against the monarch. After 15 years of war with the Turks, the royal court also concluded a peace treaty with the rebels on 23rd June 1606 in Vienna, which confirmed religious freedom.

The Protestants used this confirmation of religious freedom in the Diet to build their own church organisation in 1608. In 1610, under the protection of Palatine George Thurzo, they convoked a synod in Žilina and established a new superintendence. The counter-reformation's success was linked with the name of the archbishop Peter Pázmány, who founded a university in Trnava and converted a significant part of the Hungarian nobility back to the Catholic faith.

The nobility which won the Catholics back to their side enabled the Habsburgs to constantly break the conditions of the Vienna peace. The Transylvanian prince Gabriel Bethlen expressed his discontent with an armed uprising in 1619, when the Czech class rebellion started to escalate into a European conflict—the Thirty Years War. On 25th August 1620, he let himself be named Hungarian king by the Diet in Banská Bystrica, but not crowned. After the defeat of the Czech rebellion peace negotiations started, which ended with the signing of a peace treaty in Mikulov. Another element in the Thirty Years War was the rebellion by the Transylvanian prince George I Rákoczi, an ally of the Swedes who started military operations in Slovakia in 1644, which ended with the conclusion of a peace treaty in Linz. Religious freedom was confirmed for all Protestants, even serfs.

In the years following the Peace of Vasvár, the Hungarian nobility began to oppose the Viennese court openly. Its programmes included political, class and constitutional as well as religious demands

The movement known as Wesselenyi's conspiracy is one of the best known. When the rebel leaders' plans were disclosed, they were executed and two hundred noblemen were tried at the Bratislava court in 1671. The royal court used the Protestants' participation in the conspiracy to introduce new re-Catholicisation measures. In autumn 1673, trials of Protestant pastors and teachers accused of incitement to rebellion began. In March 1675, 41 pastors were condemned and sent to the galleys. In 1677, the discontent nobility in emigration launched an invasion on eastern Slovakia from Poland. Emerich Tököli placed himself at the rebels' head. Emperor Leopold I promised the Protestants freedom of religion at the Diet in Sopron in 1681. They were allowed to build so-called articular churches in their sees. Following the Turks' defeat near Vienna Tököli's supporters liquidated a court tribunal in Prešov (so-called Prešov massacre) in 1687.

The last anti-Habsburg uprising broke out in 1703, when the war for the Spanish succession started. Francis II Rákoczi led the rebels. The discontent nobility's conflict, with its lengthy military operations and bad economic situation, culminated at the rebel Diet in Ónod in 1707, when they killed one of the Turiec county envoys. The Diet deposed the Habsburgs. On 30th April 1711, both sides concluded a compromise peace in Szatmár.

Culture underwent sophisticated development in the modern era. Humanist and renaissance ideas came here through students from the minor nobility and bourgeoisie, who studied at Italian universities until the mid-16th century. The main intellectual flow was seen among the nobility and bourgeoisie. New religious reformation ideology, which arrived on our territory in various modifications (Lutheranism, Calvinism, Zwinglianism, Anabaptism) were spread along with humanism. In the second half of the 16th century, a Lutheran style moderate reformation based on the Augsburg Confession of 1530 gained prevalence.

The humanism, reformation and counter-reformation of the 16th century focused attention on the importance of education. Not just towns, but also the nobility and churches, established schools. Printing also stimulated the development of education in the 1570s.

Renaissance ideas had a positive influence on the development of literature. Besides the Latin work of humanist poets, historical songs describing events from battles against the Turks also assumed an important place. Love poems were also a favourite in the 16th century. There was a boom in spiritual songs in the national language as a result of the reformation. Renaissance elements prevailed in architecture at the beginning of the 16th century. Italian architects, who helped to build the anti-Turk fortresses of Komárno and Nové Zámky influenced the change in architecture and fine art. A new type of renaissance mansion started to be built as a result of the Turkish threat. Many town halls were build in the renaissance style. Town towers that stood alone were a special trademark of our architecture.

The political and religious struggles of the 17th century had an important effect on the development of education. On 12th May 1635, archbishop Peter Pázmány issued a document establishing a Jesuit *studium generale*—university—in Trnava with a faculty of theology and arts. A faculty of law was added in 1667–1668. On 26th February 1657 a *studium generale* was also established in Kosice. Piarists, Benedictines and Minorites were also active in the field of education during the counter-reformation. On 18th October 1667, a Protestant *collegium* was opened in Prešov. The Trnava and Košice universities became centres of academic life. The most famous professor at Trnava university was Martin Szentiványi.

The first atlas of the Hungarian Empire was published there in 1689 and Samuel Timon's first topographic work on Hungarian towns also originated there. At the Evangelical *collegium* in Prešov professor Izák Caban proved the existence of atoms in his dissertation. Levoča and Trnava were the main publishing centres. During the 17th century, literary work was a reflection of the social and political situation. Baroque prevailed in spiritual songs and homilies. The historical songs of the baroque period told of Turkish raids, counter-reformation battles and class uprisings. At the end of the century, prose, mainly memoirs and travelogues, became more widespread. The Jesuits organised the most theatre performances, producing more than 10 thousand school plays between 1601 and 1773.

The Road to National Emancipation

The Szatmár peace treaty of 1711 ended the period of civil wars in the Hungarian Empire. The Hungarian Diets reconciled with the Habsburg dynasty (they accepted the so-called Pragmatic Sanction, which secured the succession of the line) and this enabled them to strengthen their influence over internal developments. This was not only reflected in the reinforcement of the monarchy's power and assertion of absolutism, but also cleared the way for the introduction of measures necessary for the development of the whole society. People from the upper classes, who had often been inspired by the flow of ideas of the time—enlightenment—were best aware of their necessity and possibilities. Thanks to their initiative, various reforms gradually started to be implemented from the reign of Maria Theresa (1740–1780) and especially her sons Joseph II (1780–1790) and Leopold II (1790–1792). The reforms concerned all areas of life: the economy (the introduction of an urbarial law regulating feudal relations in 1767), judiciary (criminal law reforms), healthcare (organisation of public healthcare), education (1777 school reform). Their aim was to stimulate social and economic development and create state citizens from a population differing in social status (class), culture and confession (the 1781 Edict of Tolerance accepted the civic assertion of non-Catholics).

However, despite the efforts of Joseph II, the reforms did not reach the core of the economic system, feudal relations and privileged status of the nobility (they made up 5% of the Hungarian Empire's population) during the 18th century. Dissatisfaction that the reforms did not go far enough was expressed in the form of the so-called Jakobin movement (1792–1794). After the end of the war with France in the 1820s–30s, the Hungarian Diet also prepared reforms, but

Metternich's repressive regime and the conservatism of a significant part of the social elite prevented their realisation. Social tension and discontent over the position of the Hungarian Empire within the Habsburg monarchy led to the 1848 revolution, which ended with serfdom. Another important result was the tabling of civil rights; suffrage, freedom of the press, etc.

Slovaks also articulated their demands during the revolution, expressing their right to be recognised as a nation of Hungary with equal rights. They demanded the right to use their language in local official contact, representation in the Hungarian parliament and the development of their own education system and cultural institutions.

However, the concept of the formation of the Slovak ethnic group in the form of a modern nation clashed with the idea of the Hungarian political nation, which defined all of the state's inhabitants as one nation. Their attribute should be Hungarian, not just in the position of an official language, but also as a direct symbol of their culture and identity. The failure to address the problems of Hungary's non-Magyar nations, including Slovaks, contributed towards a split in revolutionary forces (Slovaks fought on the Austrian side against the Hungarian revolutionary guard) and eventually the revolution's defeat.

The confessional split within the Slovak ethnic group had a direct impact on the process of forming a modern nation. Its basic attribute—a codified written language—developed through the parallel use of two types of cultural language: in the Evangelicals' case this was the Czech used in the 16th century Kralice Bible (so-called Bible). In the 18th century it had become an almost canonising symbol of the Lutheran teaching's unity and stability. Its sphere of use was mainly lithurgy and theologians' books. In the circle of Catholic intellectuals, the spoken language was cultivated during the 17th and 18th centuries, which led to the codification of the so-called western Slovak cultural language by Anton Bernolák (so-called Bernolák) in 1787.

Through the dominant type of written language, Slovak intellectuals at the same time adopted historical traditions and formed an awareness of kinship with the other Slav ethnic groups. The Evangelicals formulated and cultivated a confessional affinity with the tradition of the "Czech reformation", which became a spiritual support for them in resisting re-Catholicisation and a source of pride and responsibility to help the reviving Evangelical church in the Czech lands after 1781. The concept of a Czecho-Slovak tribe (nation) as a strong part of the wider Slav nation grew from this. Its 18th century supporters were Matej

Bel, Ladislav Bartholomeides, and later Pavol Jozef Šafárik and Ján Kollár.

The cultivation of Bernolák as an attribute of the Catholic intelligentsia (Juraj Fándly, Juraj Palkovič, Ján Hollý) corresponded to the need to establish Slovaks as an independent nation with its own written language and specific past, which should participate in public life within the Hungarian Empire and could resist assimilation and its assertion by force (Magyarisation). This trend led to the adoption of a written language in 1843. The author of the grammar of written Slovak was Ľudovít Štúr, who based it on the central Slovak dialect—the "purest" language of the masses, who he regarded as the authentic bearer of the idea of the nation.

The language programme was only one of the accompanying features of the nationalist movement. The politicisation and formation of public life also played an important part. In the 1830s, associations supporting the publication of literature and culture (reader, theatre), but also focused on economic and social aims (farmers' societies, temperance societies) appeared. This politicisation was manifested in the form of defending Slovaks' rights as a nation within Hungary (petition in 1842) and abroad (publication of national defences), publishing political newspapers (1 Aug. 1845), and declaring Slovaks' demands in the Hungarian Diet (Ľudovít Štúr in 1847).

This culminated in the 1848 revolution, during which the national political manifesto was formulated in the Demands of the Slovak Nation (11.5.1848 in Liptovský Mikuláš). It defined Slovakia as an autonomous territorial unit with political representation, and the Slovak nation was to receive the right to establish its own education system up to university level and use its own flag and symbol. The leaders of the Slovaks' revolutionary movement (Ľudovít Štúr, Jozef M. Hurban, Michal M. Hodža) did not only create nationalist demands: they also supported the introduction of suffrage for all men, the abolition of censorship, the right to assembly, and the abolition of serfdom without repurchase (forfeit for landlords).

They established a Slovak National Council (16 Sep. 1848 in Vienna) to put forward their aims, which also started to organise an armed uprising. This culminated in the formation of a volunteer force, which participated in military operations at the Viennese government's side from autumn 1848 until summer 1849. They expected this to lead to the fulfilment of at least some demands, but this also meant fighting against the forces of the Hungarian revolutionary government. Their expectations from the alliance were not fulfilled and very little of the national manifesto was realised (ban on Magyarisation, limited use of Slovak in official contact).

In State Political Transformation until 1918

The introduction of a neo-absolutist regime in the monarchy in the 50s led to the repression of the Slovak emancipation movement. The ruling power did not permit political and public activity, which fundamentally determined the creation of institutional conditions for the formation of a civic society and development of national culture. The reform of the constitutional system in 1860 and 1861 did not take into account the interests and needs of non-Magyar nations in the Hungarian Empire. Therefore the Slovak National Assembly in Martin adopted the Memorandum of the Slovak Nation on 6–7th June 1861. This document expressed their basic legal and political demands: that Slovaks were recognised by constitutional actors as a distinct state-forming nation. They demanded the creation of a national self-government (autonomy) on the territory they historically inhabited, so that the Slovak language could be used in all spheres of public life. This act was led by Ján Francisci, štefan Marko Daxner and Jozef Miloslav Hurban, members of the Štúr generation.

The Hungarian Diet only functioned for a short time in 1861 and did not make any decisions on the organisation of relations between nations. The Hungarian political powers which dominated the parliament refused to address the status of non-Magyar nations on the democratic principles of equal rights. Their strategic aim was to transform the multination Hungarian Empire into a national Magyar state. Emperor Francis Joseph I, to whom the deputation turned in December 1861 under the leadership of bishop štefan Moyses with a request to issue a constitutional act establishing a national self-governing formation for Slovaks on the ethnic-territorial principle, delegated the issue of the legal organisation of national relations to the Hungarian legislative body, which renewed its activity in 1865.

The Slovak attempts at emancipation were displayed in the establishment of the cultural association Matica slovenská in 1863 and three gymnazia, where Slovak was the language of instruction. Thus, basic conditions were created for organised activity in individual areas of national culture and education.

The Austro-Hungarian Ausgleich of 1867 had a negative impact on politico-social conditions and national relations in Hungary. The Nationality Law adopted by the Hungarian Diet in 1868 prevented non-Magyar nations from becoming state-forming entities. The Magyar political elite more intensively asserted their assimilation aims and in practice systematically applied the concept of state ethnic and linguistic homogeneity.

The realisation of this state doctrine resulted in steps taken by the ruling power which led to the abolition of Matica slovenská and the Slovak gymnazia in 1874–1875. Slovaks were left without opportunities for higher education in their mother tongue and an institution whose mission was to promote cultural activity, education and scientific learning.

The Slovak National Party was established in 1871 on the basis of the Memorandum of the Slovak Nation. Its first chairman was Viliam Pauliny-Tóth, then Pavol Mudroň (1877–1914) and Matúš Dula (from 1914). After unsuccessful attempts in elections to gain a mandate, it decided on a tactic of electoral passivity in 1884. Through this approach, it protested against the nationalistic policy and electoral system in the state, because the government used illegal methods to prevent Slovak politicians from functioning in parliament. The emancipation struggle was therefore centred on the area of culture, journalism and literature, which most clearly reflected Slovak society's historical traditions and formed a platform for maintaining awareness of national independence by using Slovak.

In the 1890s, there were significant changes in Slovak society related to the processes of industrialisation, urbanisation and adaptation of the population's social structures. The political representation renewed its activities and gradually focused on forms of organised action with the aim of gaining wide public support. At the same time, co-operation was deepened with Romanian and Serbian national representatives in the interest of a common approach in the assertion of national rights. The 1895 congress of political representatives in Budapest demonstrated the Slovaks', Romanians' and Serbs' demands that their position be resolved on the basis of autonomy and federalism to create real conditions for the assertion of their national identities in the state's constitutional and political system.

From the turn of the century, Slovak policy was activated in all spheres of social life. From 1901 onwards, MPs for the Slovak National Party were voted into the Hungarian Diet and they not only worked to ensure that provisions of the Nationality Law of 1868 were fully applied in relation to non-Magyar nations, but also attained further legislation aimed at democratising public life, the political system and civil rights and freedoms.

The nature of Slovak politics was determined by its internal differences, but the realisation of the concept of national autonomy remained the strategic aim of all ideologies. Within the Slovak National Party, there was a group around its leadership in Martin which based it orientation on the continuity and traditions of the Memorandum of 1861. The most striking figure of the party's liberal wing was Vavro šrobár; Milan Hodža represented its agrarian aspect. The Slovak People's Party was created from the Catholic popular aspect in 1913 under the leadership of Andrej Hlinka. The social democrats with Emanuel Lehocký were also profiled as a separate entity from the start. Besides their specific interests, they were all based on a common fundamental national emancipation platform, consisting of the idea of Slovaks' national independence and systematically oriented on the assertion of national rights on the democratic principles of parliamentarianism and civic and national equality.

Limited voting rights excluded the majority of the population from participating in the state's administration and public affairs, which in the constitutional conditions of Hungary mainly discriminated against members of non-Magyar nations. Magyar political powers halted demands for the legalisation of universal suffrage to prevent an increase in non-Magyar nations' influence over institutions of political power and public administration. They saw this as a threat to their long-asserted Magyar national interests within the Habsburg monarchy and their position in Hungary.

At the beginning of the 20th century, the area of education became a subject of concentrated pressure from the state power, and Slovak was completely eliminated as a language of instruction in primary schools. The liquidation of Slovak education continued under the school laws of 1907 (Lex Apponyi), which provoked strong protest even abroad. The tragic events in the village of Černová in October 1907, where lives were lost at the consecration of the church due to the intervention of an armed force, received an unusually large response on a European scale.

The nationalistic policy and Magyarisation process in Hungary became a subject of criticism and condemnation in western Europe and the USA. The public there became aware of the real state of attitudes in Hungary, which evoked concern in Hungarian political circles, because Hungarian politicians' propaganda about consolidating national relations were shown to be groundless. Persecution from the power and court apparatus afflicted many organisers and activists of the national emancipation movement. The ruling regime considered the Slovak population objectionable because of their national and civil self-realisation.

The Slovak National Party officially approached the Hungarian government in June 1911 with a special Memorandum requesting that, in line with the Nationality Law, Slovak be used in primary schools, they be allowed to establish secondary schools and Matica slovenská's activity be permitted once more. The government did not respond to this initiative and so confirmed that no correction of the political line regarding Slovaks could be expected from its side.

Austro-Hungary's power-political aims and power blocs' spheres of strategic interest were followed very carefully in Slovak political circles. They counted on a possible military conflict, which could change the global constellation of the central European area and conditions for the arrangement of nationalist conditions. The need to concentrate Slovak political forces on a unified approach in the defense of national emancipation interests in case of state changes was therefore presented. From the beginning of the century, there were intensive mutual ties and co-operation between Slovak and Czech cultural and economic circles. So the background of the Slovak struggle for emancipation was reinforced outside Hungary, because the idea of co-operation gradually gained a political dimension, which was important for gaining strategic allied support on both the Slovak and Czech side.

The aim of creating a Slovak National Council in spring 1914 as a representative body containing members of every Slovak political grouping was not realised due to the outbreak of military conflict. Its establishment only became reality in the closing phase of the World War I.

Political and public life was also paralysed in Slovakia as a result of wartime conditions. However, even in the hostile atmosphere and under persecution, Slovak political circles prepared in isolation for the eventuality of changes in the state political system after the war. In September 1914 in America, the Slovak League issued a memorandum, which contained the demand of the right to self-determination for Slovaks. In connection with the submitted victory Treaty, the line of political entities of the Czecho-Slovak rebellion that the new organisation on the territory of the former Habsburg monarchy should reflect the concept of the creation of an independent state for Czechs and Slovaks started to be systematically asserted abroad. Representatives of the Slovak League and Czech National Committee signed an agreement in this spirit in October 1915 in Cleveland, USA, demanding the creation of a common independent state on the basis of a federative union of two nations.

The Czechoslovak National Council was created in Paris in 1916 as the central authority of foreign rebellion. It was led by T. G. Masaryk and its deputy chairman became Milan Rastislav štefánik. With the support of its Slovak and Czech compatriots, the council organised armed units—the Czechoslovak Legion—in France, Italy and Russia, which fought on the allied powers' side against Austro-Hungary and Germany. An agreement signed by Slovak and Czech representatives in 1918 in Pittsburgh enshrined autonomous administration for Slovakia in the future common state.

In May 1918, the Slovak political representation adopted a decision in line with the aims of the foreign rebellion to unite Slovaks and Czechs in a common state. The Slovak National Council headed by Matúš Dula was constituted and adopted its Declaration of the Slovak Nation on 30 October 1918. On the basis of the right to self-determination, it rejected Slovaks' inactivity within Hungary and stated that the Slovak nation wanted to resolve the issue of its future position on the platform of a new state created by uniting the Czech lands and Slovakia in one unit. The declaration was in line with the announcement of the creation of the Czechoslovak state on 28.10.1918 in Prague. The Slovak National Council, which declared itself Slovaks' only political representation, thereby confirmed that Slovaks were full actors in the domestic and foreign rebellion and assumed a state-forming position in the establishment of the Czechoslovak Republic.

Slovakia in the Czechoslovak Republic

The establishment of the Czechoslovak Republic on 28 October 1918 was one of the decisive breakthroughs in the history of the Slovak nation. On 30 October 1918, the Slovak National Council adopted the Declaration of the Slovak Nation, through which it entered into a common state of Czechs and Slovaks. Sub-Carpatho-Ruthenia joined a year later. The new state had an area of 140,394 km sq. and population of 13,007,831. Of this, 48,936 km sq. and 1,910,000 inhabitants belonged to Slovakia.

From the point of view of the realisation of Slovak national interests, the establishment of the Czechoslovak state was the optimal variant in the given conditions in the new European power-political arrangement. Conditions were created for free national development, the development of Slovak culture, education, and the democratisation of society, and Slovakia's borders were defined administratively for the first time. T. G. Masaryk became the first president of the common state, E. Beneš the second in 1935 and after his resignation in 1938 E. Hácha was elected as third president. The process of forming the new state was dramatic, because Hungary attempted to regain its former territory through military intervention in 1919 under B. Kuhn's Bolshevik government. After this aggression was repelled, conditions in Slovakia gradually stabilised.

The new state consisted of three politically, economically and culturally unequally developed territorial units. Their integration into a common state gave rise to a great deal of problems in all areas of social life. Moreover, numerous national minorities lived in the republic, mainly Germans in Bohemia and Moravia and Hungarians in Slovakia and Ruthenia, who were only partly integrated into the new state and were more or less opposed to it.

The Czechoslovak Republic began and developed as a pluralist democracy, which enabled the development of a rich political life. Meanwhile the republic was built as a unitarist, centralist state, where the principle of separate legislative, executive and judicial power was thoroughly applied. Immediately after the state's creation, the party political structure was renewed and in a certain sense completed in Slovakia. It included nation-wide political parties, Slovak political subjects and minority parties. Individual political subjects had significantly different views on Slovakia's status in the state. The political parties of national minorities, particularly the Hungarian minority, did not agree with the state's existence.

The prevailing majority of Czech or Czechoslovak parties saw Slovakia not as a national territorial whole, but as an administrative unit. This concept arose from the idea of a single Czechoslovak nation and was embodied in a constitutional document from 1920. In the Slovak environment, this idea was supported by state parties, mainly the social democrats led by Ivan Dérer, and the agrarians headed by Milan Hodža for a while at the beginning of the 20s. These political subjects formed a pro-government camp and represented political and economic support of the government parties in Slovakia. They inclined towards civic principles of government and represented upholders of democratic development in the Slovak environment.

The Hlinka Slovak People's Party (HSĽS) led by Andrej Hlinka and the Slovak National Party headed by Martin Rázus limited their political activity to the Slovak environment. They arose from the principle of independence of the Slovak nation and demands of autonomy under the Pittsburgh Agreement of 1918. They wanted to solve Slovakia's problems through decentralisation, the creation of a Slovak Diet and gradual assumption of political power. They elaborated a number of proposals to change Slovakia's status in the republic, the most important of which became its proposal of 5 June 1938, which requested an open federation. HSĽS was conservative/rightwing and the strongest party in the Slovak environment from 1925 (it gained 30 to 34% of the vote in elections). In the 30s, it inclined increasingly towards authoritarian forms of government.

During the 30s, political parties in Slovakia, although clearly different and for various reasons, more aggressively demanded a change in Slovakia's existing status in the state. The content of these demands went from decentralisation and the reinforcement of self-government to the federative organisation of the republic. This process was also influenced by external threats.

Czechoslovakia's international position, which stabilised in the 20s, gradually worsened following the victory of nazism in Germany in 1933. The new state searched for security guarantees in the application of collective security principles and particularly within the framework of its agreements on mutual assistance with France from 1925 and the Soviet Union from 1935. In the process of the Czechoslovak crisis of 1938, which Germany prepared and unleashed under the pretext of addressing the German minority's position in the republic, there was pressure from world powers, to which the government in Prague succumbed.

France refused to fulfil its obligations and Great Britain exerted a great deal of pressure for the Czechoslovak Republic to accept Hitler's demands. Four powers—Germany, Italy, France, and Great Britain—

signed an agreement on 29 September 1938 in Munich, which forced Czechoslovakia to relinquish large territories to Germany and Poland. Another part of this agreement was the Vienna Arbitrage of 2 November 1938, on the basis of which Slovakia had to hand over 10,390 km sq. with 859,880 inhabitants to Hungary.

The Munich agreement weakened the position of the centralist government parties. HSĽS tabled its programme of autonomy more aggressively and on 6 October 1938 in Žilina reached an agreement with some of the Slovak parties on changing the state's organisation. The republic was transformed into an asymmetric-type federation on the basis of a law on the autonomy of the Slovak land of 22 November 1938. The period of building Slovak statehood within the Czecho-Slovak Republic began.

The regrouping of political power in Slovakia led to the degradation of democratic principles and the creation of an authoritarian regime with HSĽS playing a decisive role. Within the party, its radical wing started to demand the creation of an independent state. At the beginning of 1939, Germany in particular started to support the idea of an independent Slovak state as a part of its plan to destroy Czecho-Slovakia. This pressure increased during J. Tiso's visit to Berlin on 13 March 1939. Hitler made it clear that if independence were not declared, Slovakia would be divided among its neighbours. Under this pressure, the Slovak parliament declared an independent Slovak state on 14 March 1939. The next day nazi Germany occupied the Czech lands. This temporarily dissolved the Czecho-Slovak Republic.

The creation of the common state of Czechs and Slovaks had meant the break-up of the single economic space of former Austro-Hungary. Traditional economic ties were broken and some industrial capacities were relocated abroad. Slovakia was home to 23% of Czechoslovakia's population but only 8% of its industry, and in the early decades dozens of large factories closed down: ironworks, roll mills, enamel plants, chemical factories, glassworks, textile mills. Strong competition from the developed Czech economy penetrated the open Slovak market.

High unemployment, emigration and social tension, which more than once grew into open clashes with the central power, became a lasting part of economic life in Slovakia. The stagnation of industry increased pressure on agricultural land and the number of inhabitants dependent on agriculture grew. A large section of them worked on small land holdings, which were often not large enough to make a living or increase agricultural production. A land reform of April 1919 attempted to amend land relations. Its advantage was the creation of a group of central landowners, who were able to farm efficiently on the acquired land and use modern and rationalisation measures.

The world economic crisis at the turn of the 20s and 30s affected both agriculture and industry. Its catastrophic results manifested themselves in a rapid growth in unemployment. One of the ways out of this situation was the creation of the National Economic Institute of Slovakia (NÁRUS), in which P. Zaťko and I. Karvaš participated. NÁRUS set itself the goal of resolving Slovakia's serious economic issues (industrialisation, amendment of rail tariffs, nationalisation of roads, support for the construction of technical and economic infrastructure).

A new wave of investment, mainly of Czech capital, had a favourable effect on the Slovak economy in the 30s. In the complex conditions of economic transformation following the establishment of the new state and as a result of the economic crises of 1921 and 1929, unemployment in Slovak industry reached a pre-war level in 1937. This situation made it harder to support the population and 204,000 people moved from Slovakia between the wars. The altered international situation at the close of the 30s emphasised Slovakia's geopolitical significance from the point of view of state defence and stimulated the building of industry, mainly arms production.

Despite the complex economic problems, clear progress was made in the social sphere. The eight hour working day was enacted, unemployment support, sickness and old age insurance was improved. Social legislation stood up to the toughest comparison, even on a European scale. Although the gradual pros in economic life were not clearly seen, they had significance for the future. The economic structure was supplemented and developed, transport connections completed, electrification increased productivity in industry, road networks and connections were improved, the network of monetary institutions, savings banks, insurance companies and economic co-operatives, was expanded. Slovak economic policy and interests in the 30s were defined as regional, Slovak.

Important education reform started following the end of the monarchy. By the mid-20s education had been reformed, Slovak introduced in schools and compulsory school attendance enacted. Czech professors and teachers greatly helped the building of Slovak secondary and apprentice schools and universities. In 1919, Comenius University was founded in Bratislava with faculties of arts, law and medicine, later extended by a faculty of natural science. The Technical University opened in the last year of Czechoslovakia's existence. The number of university educated Slovak intelligentsia grew thanks to the education reform and started to fulfil their cultural mission and co-act in the Slovak national emancipation process.

Conditions were created in Czechoslovakia to utilise the opportunity to study at Czech universities. A whole founding generation of Slovak science and education gained a quality university education, mainly at Prague's Charles University. The establishment of Czechoslovakia laid the foundations for the rapid cultural development of Slovakia, which was manifested in Slovak society, culture, art and education. It is hard to find similar examples of a nation developing so dynamically and universally in such a relatively short time. *Matica slovenská* and its departments of history, ethnography, linguistics, and history of literature assumed an important role in the cultivation and development of Slovak knowledge and culture. Science, art and education were also institutionally anchored in many other societies. Associations were created—the šafárik Learned Society, Circle of Academic Synthesis—which significantly influenced the development of academic thinking in Slovakia.

The Slovak National Theatre was created in 1920, and a Slovak company performed there at the beginning of the 30s. A new generation of Slovak composers and musicians appeared, in which the Music and Drama Academy in Bratislava played a significant part.

There was an unprecedented growth in literature, the number of periodicals published in Slovak increased noticeably, *Slovenské pohľady*, which dedicated a lot of space to developments in world literature, started to be published again. Slovak literary criticism entered the floor. Slovak artists, who presented their work at exhibitions abroad, assumed an important place in artistic life.

The expansion of means of mass communication also supported the favourable cultural atmosphere in Slovakia. From 1926, the broadcasting of Czechoslovak Radio in Bratislava and later Košice and Banská Bystrica disseminated education and information. The radio promoted the formation of a Slovak national identity and civic solidarity within Czechoslovakia. Film gradually became a part of cultural and artistic life. The network of cinemas was expanded in Slovakia, their number rising to around 200 by the end of Czechoslovakia's existence. Bratislava became an important cultural, administrative and economic centre, the proportion of Slovaks there increased. Regional administrative and trade centres—Košice, Prešov, Žilina, Zvolen, and Trnava, did not lose their importance. Slovakia rose from anonymity and gained clearly defined boundaries for the first time in its history.

Slovakia During the Second World War: 1939–1945

A new country appeared on the map of Europe in spring 1939—the Slovak Republic, which, however, was not created through natural national emancipation developments, but as a by-product of nazi aggression against Czechoslovakia. With its size (38,456 km sq.) and population (2.6 million), the Slovak state was among the smallest countries in Europe. And so for the first time in its history, Slovakia became a subject of international politics.

It was recognised by 27 states, but despite this the Slovak Republic's international position was uncertain and weak. The so-called Protective Treaty dictated by the nazis subordinated the new state's foreign, military and economic policy to Germany. In the hands of German diplomacy, its territory became a potential instrument in its plans to become a great power and negotiations with central European countries, which was revealed at the end of March 1939, when Slovakia was attacked by Hungary and subsequently lost a part of its territory and population.

The Slovak Republic's international position was partially stabilised shortly before the outbreak of the second world war, when it was given the role of a "model" satellite state. A logical result of this was that the Slovak Republic participated in the German aggression against Poland in September 1939. It joined the Axis power pact in November 1940, deployed its army in the war against the Soviet Union in June 1941, and even declared war on the USA and Great Britain in December 1941. These acts of war created an insurmountable obstacle to the existence of an independent Slovak state in post-war Europe, especially as all of the powers in the anti-Hitler coalition declared the reinstatement of Czechoslovakia as one of their military aims. The preservation of the Slovak Republic at that time was only linked with Germany's victory in the war. The futureless collaboration with Germany led the Slovak state into clear international isolation even during the war and invariably deepened its internal crisis.

The satellite state's political regime was built on antidemocratic principles with clear fascist traits from the outset. The totalitarianism of the regime in Slovakia had many peculiarities and cracks, and was far from being as comprehensive as in other satellite fascist countries. The head of state was president Jozef Tiso. The executive power was in the government's hands. The state's legislative authority was the parliament of the Slovak Republic, which, however, gradually degenerated. The whole of political and public life was governed and controlled by the state party—the Hlinka Slovak People's Party—which confirmed its leading position in the constitution and other laws, so that it governed not just the state's political, but its whole public life through its own party structures and the organisations it created (Hlinka Guard, Hlinka Youth, etc.). The highest executive authorities and the state party were cumulated both personally and institutionally.

There was a harsh power struggle between the conservative and radical wing inside the governing camp. The conservative camp led by president J. Tiso wanted to create a specific model of a totalitarian state with religious and corporate colouring. The fascist radicals led by prime minister Vojtech Tuka and interior minister Alexander Mach attempted to introduce a national socialist regime in Slovakia. The German leadership supported the radicals, but above all they wanted Slovakia to be a model satellite state with internally consolidated conditions and a dependable economy. Tiso's wing was a better guarantee of this, but it won over its opponents with its own weapons: by introducing the Führer principle, deepening collaboration with Nazi Germany and "solving" the Jewish issue. 90,000 Jewish citizens (almost 4% of the population) were gradually deprived of their political, economic, basic civil and eventually even human rights within this process, which culminated with the transportation of 58,000 Slovak Jews to nazi extermination camps in 1942. Another 13,000 Jewish citizens were deported or murdered in Slovakia in autumn 1944.

However, the Slovak Republic also represented the concretisation of the idea of Slovak statehood, which evoked national awareness among the majority of its population. It was also empowered by the relatively stabilised economic and social situation, which was noticeably better than in the occupied or other satellite countries of central and eastern Europe. Despite the subordination of its economic needs to Germany, the Slovak economy developed dynamically thanks to the wartime conjuncture and the fact that the war did not directly affect Slovak territory until autumn 1944. Slovakia's traditional social problem—unemployment—was eliminated. The contemporary cultural life also had relatively favourable conditions for development, although it was limited by the difficult wartime situation and ideological pressure from the totalitarian regime.

There was an anti-fascist resistance on the Slovak state's territory from the beginning of its existence. This was directly or at least ideologically linked to Czechoslovak political exiles in the West or in Moscow, which was reflected in its domestic membership and mainly in its post-war aims. The resistance took full advantage of crises inside the state, whose power and administrative authorities were increasingly infiltrated by opposition, excusatory moods from 1941. The main wings of the resistance forces were united at the end of 1943 on the basis of the Slovak National Council.

Their main political aim was to overthrow the domestic anti-democratic regime and re-establish Czechoslovakia with the unconditional recognition of the Slovak nation's separate existence and equality in the re-established state. The illegal Slovak National Council, in co-operation with resistance forces in the Slovak army, but also other state power and administrative elements, prepared an armed uprising, which broke out on 29th August 1944, when German units started to occupy Slovak territory. The Czechoslovak state was re-established on rebel territory and the Slovak National Council assumed executive and legislative power. At the beginning, the uprising seized about two thirds of Slovak territory, where 1.7 million people lived.

For two months it formed a continuous front behind the retreating German forces. Its armed force consisted of a 60 thousand strong Slovak army and 18 thousand partisans. After two months of fighting, German squads occupied the resistance's territory, but the armed resistance continued in the form of a partisan war until Slovakia's liberation from its occupiers in spring 1945.

The Slovak National Uprising started the process of the liquidation of the wartime Slovak Republic, which existed for another few months with the help of the occupying Germany army, but in almost complete international and domestic isolation. Slovakia entered the re-established Czechoslovak Republic with ambitions of being an equal political and state partner. An internal political struggle started in the renewed state about its future direction.

After the War (1945–1948). 41 Years of Communist Totality (1948–1989)

Following its liberation and the end of the second world war, Slovakia became a part of the reinstated Czechoslovak Republic led by president E. Beneš. The new power had the nature of a limited and governed democracy with contained plurality. It determined itself as a paired democracy, a so-called popular democracy, while the word popular was meant to emphasise that it was a new democracy, different from the pre-war one. It was not a totalitarian regime, but a democracy in the Soviet sphere of influence. After the war, Slovakia faced the task of reintroducing democratic principles in political and public life. But there was a problem in that the totalitarian Soviet Union was supposed to guarantee democratisation and every effort of the co-governing communist party was aimed at negating democracy and introducing it own dictatorship.

The National Front, which was a popular democratic coalition uniting all political parties, became the political basis of the new power. The process of forming a party-political structure in Slovakia culminated in spring 1946. There were four political parties: the Communist Party of Slovakia (KSS), Democratic Party (DS), Freedom Party and Labour Party. Before the war, the KSS was the countrywide organisation Communist Party of Czechoslovakia (KSČ). It was an illegal party during the war and parted with social democracy on communist principles in the Slovak National Uprising.

The unification of civic resistance groups during the uprising laid the foundations of the DS. The organisation built itself up after the changeover of the front. It was a centralist party. The Freedom Party was created in April 1946 by a splinter group from the DS. The Labour Party united social democrats who disagreed with uniting with the KSS. The KSS and DS had a decisive position, while the Freedom and Labour Parties' influence was minimal. The strongest political parties in Slovakia in the first Czechoslovak Republic—the Hlinka Slovak People's Party (HSĽS) and Republican Farmers' and Smallholders' Party (Agrarians)—could not renew their activity; these rightist conservative parties were therefore not present in the post-war party-political structures.

The new political system did not recognise opposition parties. There was no voting in the National Front. Decisions were adopted on the basis of agreements and were binding for the government, parliament, Slovak National Council and Board of Commissioners. As a result, the power and oversight function of legislative bodies was weakened. One new element in the popular democratic regime was national committees, which gradually assumed the function of state administration and self-government in districts, towns and villages and Slovak national bodies: the Slovak National Council, Board of Commissioners, commissions, and other authorities.

Slovakia entered the re-established Czechoslovak Republic as an equal partner. The leadership of the anti-nazi coalition had already sustained the legal continuity of Czechoslovakia during the war. The domestic anti-fascist resistance and new political representation spoke out in favour of the re-establishment of Czechoslovakia with an equal status for the Slovak nation. However, Slovak communists' and democrats' attempts to declare a federative state failed due to the non-concession of Czech political parties. An asymmetric type of state organisation was created—a unitarist state with state and Slovak national authorities—commissions, which had no counterpart on the Czech side. This model was at odds with the proclaimed principle of "equal with equal" and moreover the power of Slovak national authorities was gradually restricted.

After the war, Czechoslovakia re-established itself as a state of Czechs and Slovaks. It did not originally count on national minorities. It was expected that they would cease to exist due to transfers, population exchange and assimilation. The German issue was "resolved" through resettlement on the basis of a decision from the Potsdam conference of the winning powers. The Czechoslovak government lobbied for approaching the Hungarian minority in the same way. The Western powers rejected this alternative and so instead of resettlement there was only a partial population exchange between Hungary and Czechoslovakia. The other members of the Hungarian minority were given Czechoslovak state citizenship and full civil rights by autumn 1948. The development of a national education and culture was only ensured for the Ukrainian minority, but without constitutional guarantees.

The economic basis of the popular democratic regime was a three-sector economy with a public, private and private capitalist sector. It arose as a result of state interventions into the economy. In autumn 1945, key industries, large industry, banks, and private insurance companies were nationalised. There was an extensive land reform, which liquidated large estates. The land was shared by the landless and smallholders. In October 1946, the parliament approved a two-year economic plan (for 1947–1948), whose main aim was to complete the renewal of the war damaged economy. In addition to this renewal in Slovakia, the foundations of the planned industrialisation of the country were to be laid through the construction of new factories and relocation of some industry from the Czech border area to Slovakia.

The May 1946 parliamentary elections altered the share of individual political parties in power. The previous parity (equal) representation in the government, temporary parliament, Board of Commissioners, and Slovak National Council was replaced by proportional representation after the elections (each party gained a power share proportional to its election results). The DS won in Slovakia with two thirds of the vote, while just under a third of the electorate voted for the KSS. The election results for the other two parties were minimal.

The DS' victory in the elections secured it a majority in Slovak national authorities and national committees. However, this did not produce a stabilisation of political conditions in Slovakia. Since the KSČ was the winning party in the elections in the Czech part of the republic and the communists gained a small majority in parliament together with the social democrats (the communists' leader Klement Gottwald became prime minister), Slovak communists' approach to Slovak national authorities changed significantly. They stopped defending their competencies and participated in the restriction of their powers. From then on, many Slovaks saw a double danger in Prague: the threat of centralism and communism. Czech society on the other hand believed the communists' propaganda, partly also supported by civic parties, that HSĽS was rallying in Slovakia and expressing separatist tendencies.

The KSS leadership were aware that the prospect of victory in the next elections (to be held in May 1948) was unrealistic and therefore wanted to change the balance of power through non-parliamentary means. It counted on intervention from Prague and its position in unions and among former partisans. It used every opportunity to discredit the DS, which it accused of sabotaging the land reform and supplying, supporting or concealing anti-state forces. In autumn 1947, the police, which were controlled by the communists, fabricated a so-called anti-state conspiracy in Slovakia with the aim of destroying the DS. They did not succeed, but the DS was significantly weakened. By the turn of 1947/1948, the popular democratic regime was in crisis. The communists had lost interest in the National Front and were attempting to assume complete power. The civic parties on the other hand tried to keep the National Front functional and saw elections as a way out of the crisis. Their representatives were convinced that they would win the elections and the balance of power would change.

On 20th February 1948, the ministers for the Czech civic parties and Slovak Democratic Party resigned as a sign of protest against communist policy. They believed that the governmental crisis would be solved by parliamentary means. However, the communists took advantage of this in a decisive confrontation. They took control of the streets and created their owned armed units—People's Militia. On 25th February 1948, President E. Beneš accepted the ministers' resignation under pressure from the communists and the mobilised masses and prime minister K. Gottwald was able to fill the government with "his people". It was a state coup and the communist party gained a power monopoly, which was a prerequisite for building the communist regime. Czechoslovakia went from a state in the sphere of Soviet influence to a part of the Soviet bloc just as the bipolar division of the world intensified and the East and West found themselves in fierce confrontation.

In the days of the February coup of 1948 and shortly afterwards, very few people were aware of the deep political changes and their impacts. At first sight, it seemed that the changes were not large and were more about people than the system. Non-communist parties, the National Front and other pre-February institutions still formally existed. President of the republic E. Beneš continued to perform his function for several months after the coup. But in reality it meant a qualitative change of the political system, transfer of the popular democratic coalition into KSČ monopoly power, which first affected the political area and then penetrated all other spheres of social life.

The non-communist parties (in Slovakia the Freedom Party remained and the Slovak Revival Party was created from the remains of the DS) did not have the nature of real political parties and the National Front became a mere apparatus of KSČ policy. Elections no longer fulfilled their function because they were neither free nor democratic. The tight circle of KSČ leaders made decisions, not the parliament or government. The so-called "leading role of the KSČ", which was also enshrined in the constitution of 1960, was enforced in practice. The constitution also proclaimed Marxism-Leninism as the state ideology.

After the February coup of 1948, centralisation was intensified within the communist party and the whole state. The KSS became an organisational part of the KSČ in autumn 1948 and its activity completely dependent on the KSČ leadership in Prague. Within the framework of a drive against so-called bourgeois nationalism, nationally oriented communists were ousted from the KSS' leadership at the beginning of the 50s and some suffered persecution (Vladimír Clementis, Gustáv Husák, Ladislav Novomeský, etc.) Viliam Široký became its leading figure and other functionaries (Karol Bacílek, Pavol

David and others) obediently carried out orders from Prague. The asymmetric model of state organisation and increasing centralisation led to a weakening of Slovak national authorities' powers. The Board of Commissioners was abolished in 1960 and the Slovak National Council became a powerless institution, which "governed only itself".

The arrival of communist totality was accompanied by brutality and persecution. They took their most brutal form in the early years of its existence (from 1948 to the mid-50s), when the new regime pressed through fundamental changes in all areas of society following the "Soviet model". The society underwent almost non-stop purges, civil and political rights were suppressed, people were discriminated against for political, religious and social reasons. The highest form of persecution was political show trials, which were meant to evoke an atmosphere of fear and forced citizens to obey the regime implicitly. Thousands of "class enemies", church representatives, but also former partisans and resistance fighters from the war years, suffered. The most important trial politically in Slovakia was that of the so-called bourgeois nationalists (Gustáv Husák, Ladislav Novomeský and others) in April 1954, by which time such forms of persecution had already ended in other Soviet bloc states.

Shortly after the February coup of 1948, further nationalisation was carried out and the land reform continued. Essentially, the state gained control of the whole of industry, construction, wholesale and foreign trade. By the end of 1948, the KSČ leadership had started to focus on forcing out capitalist elements and transferring small businesses into "higher forms of business", i.e. state-owned businesses or co-operatives under state control. Economic pressure and administrative measures eliminated private businesses by 1953. Smallholders in the countryside also suffered a similar fate through collectivisation, i.e. the creation of co-operatives. Although officially it was emphasised that this was voluntary, in reality agriculture was mainly collectivised by force.

This transition of smallholdings into "a higher form of business" was dramatic and lasted for decades. Nationalisation, the liquidation of private businesses and collectivisation, together with the country's industrialisation (economic and social development was governed by so-called five year plans), changed the structure of Slovak society. The bourgeoisie disappeared and only a fragment of the middle classes survived. The number of employed, members of the intelligentsia and factory workers increased significantly. Society was levelled and nationalised, the economy became dependent on the state.

However, the communist regime's existence can not simply be reduced to brutality and persecution, because no dictatorship can be maintained in this way only. Many people believed the communist propaganda about a "brighter tomorrow" and visions of a society free of oppression and exploitation, with harmonious relations and lasting prosperity. The regime's economic and social policy also solved many problems from the past. The most pressing of these was the industrialisation of Slovakia, which had progressed very slowly until then. For all of its faults, the centralised economy created space for its acceleration. Thanks to this, Slovakia was transformed from a semi-agrarian to an industrial agrarian country in less than two decades. Urbanisation accompanied the industrialisation and the urban population increased. The gradual increase of investment into agriculture and inflow of qualified workers increased agricultural production, particularly after the mid-60s. The regime eliminated agrarian overpopulation and ensured a certain social security. The population became better educated and progress was made in the areas of science, healthcare and culture. But they were only relative successes and had their dark sides. The opportunities of the delayed industrialisation were not utilised and mainly heavy industry was built regardless of the economic impacts. The proportion of arms production was increased, wages were levelled, culture ideologised, and social security had a "barrack" nature.

As a result of the extensive development, the economic situation became complicated in the early 60s and the economy stagnated. The situation in the political sphere was even more complex, because the party and state leadership led by Antonín Novotný was not able to abandon the unlawfulness and reprisals of the early 50s. The situation, influenced by the de-Stalinisation in the USSR at the beginning of the 60s, forced it to review the political show trials, but only those of communist functionaries.

Meanwhile they tried to put the blame on a few "sacrificial lambs". For example, Viliam Široký, the Czechoslovak prime minister, was removed from his function, as was the KSS First Secretary Karol Bacílek. Disclosures about the trials shook the leadership's authority and increased calls for redress and reforms, criticism of KSČ policy grew. The unrest was especially strong in Slovakia, where attempts at democratic transformations were linked with the national emancipation movement and efforts to end the Slovak nation's unequal status in the state. The new leadership of the KSS (from 1963), headed by Alexander Dubček, was not plagued by the political show trials. It therefore acted more energetically than the leadership in Prague and promoted the process of democratisation. From the mid-60s, it became increasingly clear that the society had somehow woken up and abandoned its illusions and fear, and the calls for redress got louder.

At the beginning of 1968, changes were made in the leadership of the KSČ, which launched an attempt at social reform in Czechoslovakia. The compromised Antonín Novotný had to retire from the most important function in the state, first secretary of the KSČ. They replaced him with the pro-reform Alexander Dubček. This change was followed by the replacement of the president, prime minister, chairman of parliament and party functionaries on various levels. The reform started "from above", which was typical of all attempts at reform in Soviet bloc states. In April 1968, the new leadership of the KSČ submitted a reform concept called the "Action Programme", which was the most comprehensive programme of reforms of the political system in the Soviet bloc at that time. Space was created for the tabling of previously unspeakable issues, which led to dynamic societal activity.

The conservative powers linked with the past (Alois Indra, Vasil Biľak, Drahomír Kolder, and others) went on the defensive and their influence was reduced. Non-communist political parties, social organisations and churches were activated. In Slovakia, the issue of the organisation of state relations between the Czech and Slovak nation leading to the federalisation of the previously unitarist Czechoslovak state was especially topical.

The leadership of the USSR and central European Soviet bloc states watched the reform movement in Czechoslovakia with growing disapproval. Since the "warning" given to the KSČ leadership did not have the desired result, the leadership of the USSR, supported by Bulgaria, Hungary, East Germany, and Poland, decided on military intervention. On 21st August 1968 Czechoslovakia was occupied, which provoked spontaneous dissension from the population. The Czechoslovak party and state leadership condemned the occupation as an act contrary to international law. The conservative forces, relying on help from the occupying forces, were not able to form a pro-Soviet government. The Soviet leadership therefore exerted enormous pressure on A. Dubček and other reform representatives. It forced them to accept a "temporary stay" of Soviet forces on the territory of Czechoslovakia and gave the domestic conservatives unlimited support with the aim of enforcing so-called "normalisation", i.e. a return to an authoritarian style of government.

"Normalisation" started as early as autumn 1968. The conservative forces joined the so-called realists (Ludvík Svoboda, Gustáv Husák, Ľubomír Štrougal) in the battle against the reformists on a platform of recognising the military occupation of August 1968 as "international brotherly assistance". They succeeded in removing A. Dubček, the main representative of the reforms, from the post of first secretary of the KSČ in April 1969. They replaced him with G. Husák, who had been unlawfully incapacitated in the 50s and originally supported the reforms. However, in his thirst for power he did an about face and became a symbol of "normalisation" for the next twenty years.

A shake up began in the party and state apparatus. Protest demonstrations by the population on the first anniversary of the occupation were broken up by "its own forces": army, People's Militia and police units. In 1970, mass purges were carried out in the KSČ leading to the expulsion and incapacitation of supporters of the reforms. Non-members of the KSČ who disagreed with "normalisation" were also affected.

A great deal of hope was invested in the federative organisation of the state in Slovakia in 1968. A law on Czechoslovak federation was adopted in October 1968 and entered into force in 1969, but it failed to live up to expectations. In 1970–1971, federative authorities were strengthened so much at the expense of national authorities within the framework of renewed centralisation that the principles of real federation were substantially deformed.

But even in these conditions, Slovakia made progress in the 70s and 80s, although it struggled with many problems concerning the structure of industry, efficiency of production and finalisation of products. Despite all of its difficulties, it began to catch up with the more developed Czech lands in a number of important manufacturing indicators and standard of living. However, its rapid rise slowed down throughout Czechoslovakia in the mid-70s. The economic stabilisation of the "normalisation regime" helped this, but economic stagnation subsequently weakened the regime. The economy's possibilities were gradually exhausted and it was unable to grasp modern development trends.

Czech and Slovak society was divided and traumatised by the normalisation of the 70s and 80s. Besides those who benefited professionally, the "normalisation leadership" had very few active supporters. The majority of the population "adapted" and withdrew into passivity. The reformers, excluded from public life, were under police surveillance and had no opportunity to voice their opinions. The formation of an opposition with wider public support therefore met many obstacles. The belief that the model of socialism in the Soviet bloc was unreformable strengthened in the atmosphere of fear of repression. Civic groups and so-called dissident movements gradually took the initiative in the emerging opposition. The communist regime only regarded them as a fringe affair with no influence over the population and its leadership lived in the belief that it had nothing to fear from them until the mid-80s.

However, the opposition strengthened under the influence of international developments, including the situation in the USSR after M. S. Gorbachev took over. A. Dubček became active, the Catholic church and its underground structures spoke out more clearly, the green movement gained public approval. By the mid-80s, the normalisation regime had exhausted its chances of reinforcing its stability and rapidly lost not just public support, but also the support of the communist party's membership. The situation became critical and the communist regime started to fall apart.

In the Democratic World

The communist system in Czechoslovakia found itself in crisis in the late 80s. Other Soviet bloc countries succumbed to competition from the western democratic system. The democratic revolution in Czechoslovakia started on 17th November 1989. It created space for systemic changes in Slovak and Czech society influenced by Soviet Perestroika and the fall of the Berlin Wall. The transformation of the social system also arose as a result of the communist regime's suppression of the 1968 Prague Spring through twenty years of normalisation policy. 17th November 1989 was a historic milestone in Czechoslovakia's and Slovakia's history. It was connected with the establishment of a democratic system.

The "velvet" revolution started with the suppression of a student demonstration in Prague on 17th November. Students had already protested in Bratislava the day before. The revolution's main demands included freedom of the press, the observance of human rights and freedoms, the removal of the leading role of the KSČ from the constitution, the de-ideologisation of education and culture, equality in law of all forms of ownership, the establishment of the rule of law, and a real democratic federation.

The Federal Assembly cancelled article 4 of the Constitution of the ČSSR on the leading role of the KSČ through a constitutional law. The occupation of Czechoslovakia in August 1968 was condemned as illegal, wrong and unjustified. The communist regime's main document of the "normalisation" policy—Lesson From the Crisis Development in the Party and Society Following the Thirteenth

Congress of the KSČ—became invalid. One of the regime leading representatives, president Gustáv Husák, resigned. Václav Havel, a representative of the new political power in the Czech lands—Civic Forum—became the new president. The central figure of the 1968 Prague Spring, Alexander Dubček, became chairman of the Federal Assembly.

The hand-over of power from the pragmatic communists to democratic forces, mainly represented by Public Against Violence, was carried out peacefully in Slovakia. Rudolf Schuster became chairman of the Slovak National Council and Milan Čič Slovak prime minister. The political reconstruction of the Federal Assembly and national councils enabled the adoption of key legislation on citizens' fundamental rights and freedoms and a pluralist political a economic system. Parliamentarianism was renewed. Slovak and Czech civic society was formed.

The face of Slovak society changed. New political parties and movements appeared and some which had disappeared following the state coup in February 1948 were re-established. The largest political entities included the Christian Democratic Movement, Slovak National Party, Green Party in Slovakia, Democratic Party, social democracy, and Hungarian political entities. The Slovak communists underwent a process of transformation into a modern left-wing social democratic type party. The nationalities' status was addressed. Relations between the Czech and Slovak nations started to be resolved on the principles of equality, equality in law and autonomy in democratic conditions.

Slovakia received a new name the Slovak Republic. But in spring 1990, a dispute broke out between the Czech and Slovak political representation over the equal status of the Slovak Republic with the Czech Republic in the common state's name and state symbol of the Czechoslovak federation. The name Czech and Slovak Federative Republic was adopted. The basic political, national, property, civic, and economic aims of the democratic revolution in Czecho-Slovakia were fulfilled in the parliamentary elections in June 1990. Public Against Violence won in Slovakia. The election results showed that the citizens of Slovakia had decided in favour of a democratic system and the end of the communist dictatorship.

The system was changed through reforms in ownership relations and the economy, education, the legal system, healthcare, the social system, and public administration. Privatisation and the rehabilitation of all population groups acquired substantial dimensions. There were changes in the orientation of foreign and security policy. As early as February 1990, the government adopted a decision on Czecho-

Slovakia's withdrawal from the Council of Mutual Economic Assistance. The ČSFR was accepted as a full member of the Council of Europe a year later. The Czecho-Slovak state's sovereignty was renewed with the Soviet army's withdrawal. The Warsaw Pact was dissolved and Czecho-Slovakia developed initiatives to join NATO. It signed a large number of international agreements, and not just with neighbouring states. International relations gained a different nature to the period before November 1989.

However, Slovakia was burdened by disputes with Hungary over the Gabčíkovo-Nagymaros Dam.

Resolving the Czecho-Slovak state's status on new democratic principles was one of the key problems faced by Slovak and Czech society after the elections. Two different concepts were put forward: Czech representatives lobbied for a more centralist federation with powerful federal authorities, the Slovaks more for strong national republics. The adoption of the so-called competency law in December 1990, which amended the deformed federation of December 1970, drew the dividing lines in the Czecho-Slovak federation and its relation to the national republics. However, the disputes over the organisation of legal relations between the Slovak and Czech nations continued. There were also differences of opinion on the signing of agreements or treaties between the Slovak Republic and Czech Republic. In November 1991, the federal government submitted a proposal for a centralist federation. The Slovak national authorities opposed this and did not adopt the draft agreement on the principles of the legal organisation of the common state of February 1992. Further attempts to reach a political agreement between the Slovak and Czech representation also failed.

The parliamentary elections in summer 1992 showed that the winners—the Civic Democratic Party headed by Václav Klaus in the Czech lands and Movement for a Democratic Slovakia led by Vladimír Mečiar in Slovakia—differed in their concepts for the common state's organisation. At talks in Brno, Bratislava and Jihlava they decided to dissolve the Czech and Slovak Federative Republic as of 1st January 1993. The Slovak National Council adopted the Declaration of the Slovak National Council on the Sovereignty of the Slovak Republic on 17th July 1992. On 1st September 1992, it adopted the Constitution of the Slovak Republic under the number 460/1992 Coll. On 25th November 1992, the Federal Assembly of the ČSFR adopted a constitutional law on the dissolution of the ČSFR as of 31st December 1992. The peaceful split of the Czecho-Slovak federation led to the creation of two independent states. On 1st January 1993, the Slovak Republic was created as an independent, sovereign and democratic state. It had become a fully-fledged member of the international community.

Government

The Government and Political System in Slovakia

Slovakia is a democratic republic. It is a parliamentary, multi-party system. The government is divided into 3 branches, the executive, legislative and judicial branch.

The President is the head of state and is elected by direct, popular vote using a two round system for a five year term. The executive head however, has very limited powers. Most executive power lies with the prime minister who is appointed by the president and who is usually the leader of the majority party or coalition. Ministers or members of the cabinet are also appointed by the president based on the recommendation of the prime minister.

The National Council of the Slovak Republic occupies the legislative branch. It is a unicameral body composed of one hundred fifty seats.

Members are elected based on proportional representation and serves for a 4-year term. This body concerns itself with the constitution and its statutes and other legal acts. They also approve all important international treaties before ratification.

The Constitutional Court of Slovakia is the highest body of the judicial branch. The thirteen seats of the court are filled in by presidential appointment from a list of candidates nominated by parliament. As the name implies they issue rulings on constitutional issues. The Supreme Court is the highest appellate forum of the country. Under these two are the regional, district and military courts. In 2002, a judicial council was created by parliament. It is composed of eighteen members who are either judges, law professors or other legal experts. Its purpose is to nominate judges except for the constitutional court and also to appoint disciplinary senates for probing judicial misconducts.

Education system

Education in Slovakia is currently ranked as having one of the best in the world up to the secondary level. Currently, Slovakia's secondary education system is ranked as Number 30 in the world, next to the United States. 99% percent of the citizens of Slovakia aged 15 and above can read and write. Literacy rate among Slovakians is among the highest in the world because the government imposes to all citizens to attend school for at least nine years. Elementary education is only 4 years while secondary education is 8 years. Compulsory education is only up to the 4th year of the secondary level and after that, the student may pursue a job or pursue higher studies.

Being compulsory, that means the government is shouldering the costs of education, and in fact, education expenditures have amounted to 3.9% of total GDP from 2005 figures which ranks Slovakia 111th in the world in terms of expenditure but then again Slovakians belonging to the age group of 0-14 roughly totals about 900,000 only and so the government is really actually spending a lot in its drive to educate the masses and making sure they get quality education. In fact ratio of students per teacher is at 20 students per 1 teacher.

In 2006, Slovakia has registered 8.9% increase in GDP, one of the highest in Europe and appears to be sustaining the growth. This growth has been attributed to the high literacy rate of the region attracting unprecedented foreign investments. As evidenced by its bustling economy, the government is truly to be applauded for investing in the education of its citizenry.

With all the economic barometers giving positive results to better things to come, and as a testimony to Slovakia's economic miracle, the country has now an aid provider status.

Health & safety
Health Care, Disease Control, Crime and Safety in Slovakia

Slovakia provides quality health care. They have several big and specialized hospitals located in major cities like Bratislava, Kosice, Martin and Banska. They also have one hospital and several health centers in each city. All in all, Slovakia has a total of 78, polyclinics, 84 hospitals, and 23 specialized institutes. The nurse per population ratio is also higher as compared to other European country. They have emergency numbers that are available for medical situation that needs urgent care. There are several pharmacies in each town and cities and is generally open from 7:30 am until 4:00 in the afternoon.

Slovakians use health insurance to pay for their healthcare. It is the obligation of each citizen to pay their medical insurance, which is being deducted from their wages. The Slovakian government pays for the citizens who are exempted from making any contribution like the unemployed, the elderly and citizens with long-term disease and disability. Not all medical expenses are covered though like for example cosmetic surgery and dental treatment. This kind of procedures the patients have to cover the full payment by themselves. They have five health insurance companies responsible for the collection of the contribution and reimbursements of benefits.

The water is fluorinated and is safe to drink, but the people in Slovakia are also very fond of bottled water. The immunization rate in this country is remarkably high which only shows how aware the Slovakians health wise. The HIV/AIDS prevalence is very low with a ration of 0.01% per 100 adult.

Economy

The Economic Activity of Slovakia

In March 2008, Slovakia was written off in World Bank's list of aid recipients. Now, this can only mean one thing, the economy must be doing very well. In fact, Slovakia is now a member of Organization for Economic Co-operation and Development (OECD) where members are countries with high income economies and more recently was also admitted to the European Union. Because of this turn of events in Slovakia, this landlocked country is now referred to as the "Tatra Tiger."

Basically, Slovakian economy revolves around services, automotive manufacturing and electrical engineering. Car makers such as Volkswagen, Peugeot Citroen and Kia Motors main manufacturing plants are in Slovakia and have contributed a total output of 571,071 cars in 2007 alone. Sony's LCD TVs, Samsung's computer monitors and

Television sets which are sold all over the world are also being produced in Slovakia.

Thanks to the government's thrust of privatizing formerly government-controlled companies or industries, and is now nearing 100% completion, the economy is registering sustained growth year on year since 2001. In 2006, the country's GDP annual growth reached 8.9%, the highest among OECD member countries for that year, and as of 2007 registered 10.4%. Unemployment, although is high among European standards, have declined greatly from 2001 figures of 19.3% to 13.4 in 2006. Inflation is also indicative of good tidings as it was kept at bay at 4.3% as compared to 2003 figures of 8.4%. Another indication that Slovakia is indeed doing right in terms of managing their economy is that it has reduced its foreign debt from 49% of its GDP to 30.4%.

People and Culture
The Culture, Traditions, and Heritage

One of the fast becoming famous tourist destinations in Europe now is Slovakia. Typically, one would think that Slovakia is a laid back country and that people are still lining up on food queues to get their rations. However, thanks to political and economic reforms instituted, a country that was under communism 2 decades back is now a capitalistic advanced economy.

One remarkable thing about Slovakia is that it gives total religious practice freedom to anyone. Slovakia is generally characterized by Roman Catholics with 60.4% of the population of 5 million adhering to its doctrines, 9.6% are atheists or doesnâ€™t practice any religion at all, 5% are Eastern Orthodox and 19% are classified as others.

With regards to politics, Slovakia has a parliamentary democratic form that allows for a multi-party system. They vote a president as head of state who in turn appoints a prime minister who runs the government.

Although all of Europe are fanatics of soccer, Slovakians are more in love with the sport, ice hockey. In fact, a lot of players in the NHL, the premier league in the world of hockey, are Slovaks and so whenever there's a game of hockey shown live expect the bars getting noisier than usual as they cannot help but root for their countrymen.

When it comes to food, there is really nothing they can call their own yet like when you say an Italian or French cuisine but a typical traditional Slovak would have potatoes, cheese, bread, cabbage, onions as bases of traditional food and would generally eat pork, beef, chicken and fish for meat. Famous must-try Slovakian concoction is the bryndzove halusky, dumplings made from potato with sheep cheese and scrambled bacons for toppings.

Slovakians are also art lovers. They love to go to theaters and museums which their country is plenty of. They have a rich folk tradition as Slovakian's history of suppression forced them into it and also because of its mountainous terrain, which by the way are now becoming popular ski resorts.

Right now, the Slovak culture is really hard to characterize as their sovereignty as a nation is in its infancy stage and political and economic reforms is a work in progress. Who knows, 5 to 10 years from now, Slovakia could be the center of trade in Europe.

Religion

Religious Beliefs and Spirituality in Slovakia

Christianity is the main religion in Slovakia. This is quite evident based on the numerous churches of various faiths that can be found in the cities and villages. The beginning of Christianity in Slovakia can trace back its roots up to the first century AD. The first Christian church was built in 833 A.D. in the city of Nitra.

There is freedom of religion in the Slovak Republic, their constitution guarantees it. Based on current census, there are almost 70% Roman Catholics, 10% Protestants, 4% Greek Catholic or Eastern Orthodox, 3% belong to others religions and 13% who have none. Aside from the abovementioned the other religious denominations are the Augsburg, Reformed Christian, Czech and Slovak Orthodox, Jehovah's Witnesses, Methodist, Baptist, Seventh Day Adventist, Apostolic Hussite Church and other smaller denominations of various faiths. There was a substantial Jewish population before the Second World War. However Nazi genocidal policies have reduced their numbers to around two thousand.

There are also Catholic primary and secondary schools as well as universities. Religion is a subject in the primary schools but parents can choose other subjects like Ethics as an alternative. Some television stations have regular broadcasts of programs with religious themes. Some of these religious groups also published their own newspapers magazines and books.

The Roman Catholic Church has eight dioceses including three archdioceses. The Eastern Orthodox followers are mostly staying in the Ukrainian or Ruthenian areas which are located in the north and south of the country.

Languages

The official language of Slovakia is Slovak. It is a descendant of the Proto-Slavic language which itself also derived its origins from the Proto-Indo-European. It is closely related to Western Slavic mainly Czech and also share similarities with other Slavic languages, particularly Southern Slavic and Old Church Slavonic. Influences from Latin, Hungarian, German and English further enriched the Slovak tongue.

While majority of the population speak Slovac, other languages are used especially by the ethnic minorities. Because the republic was once a part of the former Czechoslovakia, Czech is widely understood here. The largest of the ethnic minorities are the Hungarians who mostly lived in the southern part. They speak and write in Hungarian.

The Roma or Gypsies who are the second largest minority group speak in Romani. Some of those who live near the borders of Poland and Ukraine speak in Polish and Ukrainian respectively. The Rusyns or Rusins who lived in the Eastern part, the Carpathian Mountains in particular, also have their own language. There is a German community and a number in the population who can speak in German. Russian was a compulsory subject in school until 1989. Still many adults can communicate in Russian. English is gaining quite a following in Slovakia with the young people as its most enthusiastic speakers.

In 2009, the State Language Law of Slovakia underwent a major amendment. It contains a declaration that the Slovak language has priority above all the others spoken in the country. Penalties in the form of fines will be issued to its citizens who will not use Slovak as prescribed by law despite repeated written notices.

Gastronomy
Food, eating habits and cosine of Slovakia
Though it differs from one region to another, Slovakian diet traditionally consists of pork, poultry, milk, cheese, potato and cabbage. There are many local delicacies that will surely be a treat to your taste buds. One of the most famous dishes in Slovakia is bryndzovÃ© haluÅjky, a potato dish topped with fried bacons. It can

be enjoyed in most local restaurants in Slovakia. Bryndzové halušky means sushi in Japanese and pizza in Italian. Restaurants do use rice although it is not grown in Slovakia and is imported from another country.

Breakfast usually consist of various kinds of bread with butter, cheese, ham or sausage, and even jam and honey. Lunch is served between 11 am to 12 noon. The main meal can either be meat or poultry, pasta, and is usually served with soup like Goulash which is made of beef, potatoes, paprika and marjoram.

Beer is very popular with both old and young Slovakian. There are different types of beers coming from the different region in Slovak. Wine is also being consumed by many and the most well-known is the Tokaj wine from the Tokaj region. For those who prefers non-alcoholic beverage, they have vinea which basically a grapes juice, all-natural with no synthetic or artificial flavoring. Slovakian people also love coffee. They go out for coffee as much as they go out to have a beer.

Slovakian diet is surely a very interesting treat. It does not matter where you come from, you will find a meal that will be a reminder of home and is truly satisfying.

Travel and Tourism

Travel Guide

From the Roman Empire to Greater Hungary, to the smaller half of the Communist nation of Czechoslovakia, the Slovak Republic has spent most of its long history under the rule of much larger empires. Its 1993 Velvet Divorce from Czechoslovakia was only the third time in 2,000 years that this tiny territory became an independent nation. The country's two other independence periods were a brief time during WWII and a point during the Great Moravian Empire, which lasted between the 5th and 10th centuries.

The Slovak Republic is still developing as both an independent nation and tourism destination, but this tiny country has become an increasingly popular stop for many people during tours of nearby Hungary, Austria, and the Czech Republic. Its capital, Bratislava, may not yet boast as many tourists as Prague or Vienna, but this smaller city formerly known as Pozsony ranked among the most powerful in

Europe during its over 300 years as Greater Hungary's capital. The 16th century Bratislava Castle has only recently been reopened after a decades-long restoration project which started in the 1950s, while the Devin Castle has seen centuries of trading activity from its location at the one-time border of the Iron Curtain where the Danube and Morava rivers intersect.

However, only a handful of the Slovak Republic's countless ancient castles are located in Bratislava. Visitors must venture outside the city to admire the country's best preserved castles, most beautiful wooden churches, and most accessible cave complexes, the longest of which is approximately 15 miles long. The Low Tatras ski resort of Jasna has quickly become a cheaper and less crowded alternative to several Alps skiing spots. Tatras National Park's mountains, Pieniny National Park's outstanding rafting, and Mala Fatra National Park's endless beach forests are just a handful of the surprisingly diverse landscapes found within this relatively tiny nation.

Slovakia's hottest region is near its national capital, Bratislava, where summer temperatures can soar up to 99°F and hover around 68°F long after dark. November to February is the period containing the vast majority of snowfall during Bratislava's winters, snowfall forms about 20 percent of the country's annual precipitation. The country's more mountainous regions experience colder, longer, and more severe winters, while the Slovak Republic's basins experience similar cold winters and cool summer temperatures.

Hotel rooms can be tough to find in the Slovak Republic, especially during the peak summer, skiing, and holiday seasons. Booking as much as a year in advance is recommended in many cases. Camping is also commonly available, and visitors can even stay in private guest homes. Bratislava contains a few youth hostels. However, the country's most relaxing places to stay may be its more than 94 destination spas, many of which have welcomed guests for well over a century. Slovak cuisine, like so many other aspects of the country's culture, is heavily influenced by neighboring Germany, Austria, and Hungary.

Although Bratislava Milan Rastislav Štefánik Airport is the country's largest air gateway, it currently offers no direct flights to North American cities. Many North American visitors find it more convenient to fly into the nearby Vienna International Airport and then travel the 34 miles to Bratislava by car, bus, or rail. Bratislava has become an increasingly frequent stop on Danube River cruises and Rail Europe journeys across the continent. The Slovak Republic is within easy driving distance of at least four other European nations, and its road quality is on par with that of its neighbors. Rail travel across the nation is generally quicker and cheaper than bus travel, but buses travel to a greater number of places.

Things to Do

A high percentage of the Slovak Republic's active pursuits are found among the High Tatras, Eastern Europe's only mountain range. The country's oldest national park is named after this stunning mountain range which transforms itself seasonally into a winter skiing getaway and summer rock climbing location. Guided hiking and cycling tours across the republic take visitors past some of Europe's best-preserved, centuries-old castles and most accessible ancient caves.

In the eastern Slovak Republic, the landscape dramatically changes from High Tatras peaks to the rolling highlands near the Dunajec River, where visitors can go whitewater rafting along the country's border with Poland. Many of the experienced instructors who lead the guided group floats along the river between April and October are dressed in traditional folk costumes.

Most leading Slovak Republic tour companies, including *Travel Slovakia* and *Best Slovakia Tours*, offer guided hiking tours whose difficulty levels range from leisurely strolls through Bratislava to challenging treks across the High Tatras. It takes between five to six hours for most people to hike one of the Slovak Republic's most beautiful trails, the Magistrale, between Starý Smokovec, the Sliezsky Dom mountain lodge, and Tatranská Polianka railway station.

The High Tatras is also the Slovak Republic's prime rock climbing destination. *Slovak Mountain Guide* offers rock climbing lessons by qualified instructors prior to rock climbing excursions through one of the world's smallest, yet most beautiful, mountain ranges. The 8,710 foot high Gerlachovsky Mountain is merely the tallest of the 25 High Tatras peaks towering more than 8,200 feet above sea level.

Luka is one of the few Bratislava agencies that rents bicycles to tourists wanting to take scenic cycling tours across the Slovak Republic's historic capital. Cyclists can pedal directly from the Luka office to Železná Studienka Park, then take their bicycles up the chairlift before riding back downhill. Cyclists can also follow the Danube River for less than five miles across far flatter terrain to the historic Devin Castle.

Rafting Pieniny is just one of many whitewater rafting operators based in the eastern Slovakian community of Cervený Klástor, the starting point of many guided group Dunajec River floats which travel over seven miles to the Pieniny National Park community of Lesnica and feature guides wearing traditional folk costumes from the highlands.

Although only a dozen of the Slovak Republic's over 3,800 caves are open to the public, nearly all of the country's accessible caves are included in the guided caving expeditions that *Tatrawell* provides. This local company's expert spelunkers explain the caves, their creation, and the species that live in them in great detail. The Slovak Republic's longest cave complex is about 15 miles long, and all of the country's caves are official national treasures.

Sakertour, which includes the Slovak Republic on its central European bird watching tour itinerary, caters to visitors who would rather watch the rare bird species soaring above the country's skies than explore its underground caves. Bird watching tour participants are encouraged to pay as much attention to the calls of the country's birds as the skies where these winged creatures fly.

Mlyn J.R.I. and *Osada Dallas* are two Slovak Republic stables offering guided horseback riding tours, many of which include accommodation in peaceful villages. Visitors can learn about the breeding process on horse farms or sample some of the products made at traditional salash mountain sheep corrals.

Skiing tops the list of popular winter offerings on *EST Frontier Slovakia* and *RAJEC Travel* itineraries. Jasna, the Slovak Republic's biggest ski resort, is situated in the heart of the Low Tatras. However, less experienced skiers may feel safer soaring down the four beginner and intermediate runs at Strbske Pleso. The bigger Tatranska Lomnica boasts a greater variety of runs, ranging from beginner level to a challenging expert run that spans over half a mile down a 7,204 foot high mountain. Costs and crowds are both far smaller in the Slovak Republic's ski resorts than in the Alps.

Attractions

The Slovak Republic is a land loaded with unique wooden churches, some of Europe's best preserved castles, thousands of caves, and relaxing thermal spas. Devin Castle is just one of eight different buildings scattered throughout the Slovak Republic's capital which belong to the Bratislava City Museum, but the city's better known namesake castle boats the best Bratislava views. However, no Slovak Republic castle stands higher than eastern Slovakia's 650 foot high Spissky Hrad. A remote community called Medzilaborce is home to the Warhol Family Museum of Modern Art, dedicated to the famous American pop artist whose family moved from eastern Slovakia to the United States before he was born.

Bratislava Castle (Bratislavský Hrad)
Views of Bratislava, Austria, and even Hungary await visitors who climb to the top of the capital's namesake 16th century castle, which

stood in ruins for nearly 150 years between the time it was burned to the ground in the 19th century and the beginning of a decades-long restoration during the 1950s. Four entrance gates guard the main castle building where a 262-foot deep well stands in the middle of the courtyard. The castle also houses a music hall within its former Baroque chapel, the National Council of the Slovak Republic, and the Slovak National Museum. Address: n/a Phone: n/a Website: n/a

Spis Castle (Spissky Hrad)
The largest of the Slovak Republic's countless medieval castles towers 650 feet high above the Spis region's cliffs. This early 13th century castle, still among the biggest in central Europe, once belonged to royalty and ranked among Europe's most significant Gothic castles. Although much of this national monument remains in ruins, visitors can easily imagine how it looked during its prime at the small museum which depicts its history.Address: Spissky Hrad, 05304 Spišské Podhradie Phone: +421 053 454 1336
Website:http://www.spisskyhrad.sk

Andy Warhol Museum of Modern Art
Legendary American modern artist Andy Warhol never saw his ancestral home of Medzilaborce, which his parents left for the United States prior to his birth. However, Warhol's fame has extended much longer than 15 minutes at his namesake museum, the main attraction

at this eastern Slovakian community near the Polish border. The museum proudly displays some of Warhol's most famous works, including two of his Campbell's Soup paintings and his Vladimir Lenin portrait. Address: Andyho Warhola 749/26, Medzilaborce, Slovenská republika 068 01 Phone: +421 57 74 800 72 Website: http://www.andywarhol.sk/

Tatras National Park (Tatranský Národný Park)
No Slovak Republic national park has a longer history than this one, which encompasses Eastern Europe's sole alpine mountain range, among the smallest on Earth. Bears and mountain goats frolic freely along the slopes of this winter skiing and summer hiking paradise. The lower slopes of the High Tatras are covered with pristine bodies of water and dense forests. Much of the High Tatras' diverse landscape, plant life, and wildlife is exhibited at the on-site TANAP Museum. Address: Tatranský Národný Park, Tatranska Lomnica Phone: +421 52 446 7195 Website: http://www.tanap.sk/

Pieniny National Park (Pieninský Národný Park)
This national park extending across the border to Poland may be the Slovak Republic's smallest, but a large amount of beautiful landscape is included within its borders. The park's main attractions are Červený Kláštor's Museum of National Culture, the Dunajec River Gorge's whitewater rafting, and its namesake Pieniny Mountains. More than

760 butterfly species fly above Pieniny National Park. Address: Pieninský Národný Park, Červený Kláštor Phone: +421 52 418 10 713 Website: n/a

Mala Fatra National Park (Malá Fatra Národný Park)
Storks and eagles soar above this Malá Fatra mountain park whose scenic landscape is approximately 83 percent covered in beech forests. The Šútovo Waterfall towers nearly 125 feet above the Jánošíkove diery's stunning canyons and gorges, the historic Strecno and Starhrad castles, and the calcite-encrusted Crystal Cave beneath the Malý Rozsutec Mountain. The park's boundaries also include the picturesque villages of Terchová, Štefanová, and Podšíp. Address: Správa NP Malá Fatra, Hrnčiarska 197, Varín Phone: +421 41 507 1411 Website: http://www.npmalafatra.sk/

Devín Castle (Devínsky Hrad)
The ancient Devin Castle, now one of eight Bratislava City Museum branches throughout the Slovak Republic's capital, is perched nearly 700 feet above the meeting place of the Morava and Danube rivers. Humans have lived in, and fought over, this strategic trading site since Neolithic times. The oldest known Christian church north of the Danube was founded among the ruins of a Roman fort which stood in this spot before the current castle was established in the 8th century. During the Cold War, barbed wire and watchtowers surrounded this

castle on the border between Austria and the country then known as Czechoslovakia. Several imprisoned maidens were said to have jumped to their deaths from the tiny Maiden Tower, the smallest of the castle's towers. Address: Muránska ul., 841 10 Bratislava Phone: +421 2 65 73 01 05 Website:

http://www.muzeum.sk/default.php?obj=hrad&ix=hd_mm...

Bratislava City Museum

The biggest of Bratislava's many museums is actually a network of eight different buildings scattered throughout the Slovak Republic city. The Museum of the City History is the main museum, first established in 1868 and situated close to the main square of Bratislava's historic Old Town Hall. The House of the Good Shepherd's clock museum, the arms and city fortifications museum inside the Michael's Gate tower, and the ancient Devin Castle are also part of the Bratislava City Museum. This museum network also contains museums dedicated to Johann Nepomuk Hummel, Arthur Fleischmann, and Janko Jesenský, as well as Rusovce's Gerulata National Cultural Monument. Address: Organizace Múzeum Mesta Bratislavy, Radničná ul. č. 1, 81518 Bratislava Phone: +421 2 591 008 12 Website:

http://www.muzeum.bratislava.sk/en/

Holidays and Festivals

This typically reserved nation lets down its hair several times per year during the Slovak Republic's numerous folk festivals and national holidays. The good times begin on New Year's Eve, one of the busiest Slovakia holiday seasons, and last until the month-long Christmas markets close on city streets. The picturesque Krivao mountain village of Východná hosts the largest of all the Slovak Republi'sc folk festivals, while the ancient Bojnice Castle supplies the stunning backdrop for the International Festival of Ghosts and Monsters.

Sled Dog World Championships Sprint
Each February, the Slovak Republic mountain village of Donovaly hosts one of Europe's most competitive dogsled races. While some of the world's best dog-sledders mush across the Starohorské Vrchy, the Low Tatras, and the Veľká Fatra mountains, attendees can enjoy attractions, refreshments, and live country music nearly 3,150 feet above sea level.

International Festival of Ghosts and Monsters
The 12th century Romantic Bojnice Castle provides the perfect setting for this annual ghosts and monsters festival which attracts over 50,000 visitors between April and May each year. Audience participation is strongly encouraged during this monster-filled festival which is centered around a different story, characters, and ideas every year.

Visitors can also encounter alien invasions, witches, vampires, tragic romances, and stalls loaded with food and refreshments.

Košice Music Spring Festival
The biggest music festival in the Slovak Republic's second biggest city also happens to be among the country's oldest music festival. Both the Czech and Slovak philharmonic orchestras make beautiful music during this week-long May classical music festival which was first held in 1956. The festival also attracts chamber orchestras, opera performers, and other talented classical musicians.

Junifest
The constant flow of suds may be the biggest attraction for many people at this 10-day long Bratislava beer festival, but drinking is not the only enjoyable attraction offered here. More than 300 musical performances are on this June festival's bill each year alongside games, food, and raffle ticket draws for wonderful prizes.

Východná Folklore Festival
Dozens of traditional folk festivals are held in the Slovak Republic each year, but none can rival the size of this lively celebration in the picturesque village of Východná beneath the Krivao Mountains. This festival, held over three days during the first weekend of July every year since 1953, now attracts up to 1,500 performers and 70,000 spectators on an annual basis. Folk dancing, singing, and crafts are the

festival's main attractions. Many Východná residents even welcome festival attendees into their own homes during the festival.

Coronation Ceremonies
These elaborate three-day long ceremonies are a throwback to Bratislava's more than three centuries as Greater Hungary's capital, when 11 Hapsburg monarchs received their crowns within the city's Dome of St Martin. Although the Hapsburgs no longer rule the land, their majestic era lives on during this September coronation re-enactment complete with horseback riding processions, shooting demonstrations, folk festivities, and actors taking the king's oath on the very spot where the monarchs first ascended their thrones.

Salamander Days
This early September weekend festival is the biggest event in the Slovak Republic's most attractive mining town, Banská Štiavnica. Both the festival and its closing Salamander Procession are named after the wooden lizard the chief shepherd holds in his hand while telling stories about the origin of the mines. Mine-dwelling dwarfs called *bergmans* follow the chief shepherd while bearing mining flags to the sounds of mining music. This festival is a tribute to the Slovak Republic's many miners, oilmen, and ironworkers.

Apple Festival

The humble apple is the major star of this October festival held within a medieval castle yard in the orchard community of Modra, just a 30-minute drive away from Bratislava. Several different kinds of freshly picked apples, apple seeds, and apple products are ready to be sampled and purchased each fall. The festival also contains children's games and apple preparation competitions between teams of between two and four people.

Food and Restaurants

Traditional Slovak cuisine is hearty and loaded with influences from neighboring Hungary, Austria, and Germany. Although each region has its own unique dishes, the country's unofficial national food is *bryndzové halušky*, potato dumplings filled with *bryndza*, fermented sheep cheese. Most restaurants garnish their *bryndzové halušky* with bacon pieces. The most frequently found restaurants in the rural northern Slovak Republic are called *salas* after the sheep farms from which several city restaurants obtain their ingredients. Italian, Chinese, and Vietnamese are the nation's most popular international cuisines. The most common local drinks are a strong gin called *borovicka* and a plum brandy named *slivovica*.

Bars and Pubbing in Slovak Republic

Although virtually every Slovak social event involves alcohol and the legal drinking age of 18 is rarely enforced, traditional Slovak watering holes have become increasingly hard to find in Bratislava. However, the capital contains a large amount of modern nightlife within its Old Town, where parties begin between 10:00 p.m. and 11:00 p.m., and usually do not end until 1:00 a.m. or 2:00 a.m.

Many Bratislava nightclubs are perched high above the Danube River, including the city's most crowded night spot, *Cirkus Barok* (Rázusovo nábreie 2, Bratislava). This three-level Danube River barge hosts a wide variety of live performances and themed parties. The *Slovak Pub* (Obchodná 62, Bratislava) is one of Bratislava's biggest and most relaxing watering holes. Bratislava's European Union representative office just happens to stand next door to an authentic Belgian beer café called *Café De Zwaan* (Panská 7, Bratislava).

Kosice's most sophisticated cocktail bar is *Cosmopolitan* (Kovácska 9, Kosice), which occasionally hosts champagne tastings. *Jazz Club* (Kovácska 39, Kosice) has been the leading music club in the Slovak Republic's second biggest city for years, but despite its name, jazz is far from the only type of music performed here.

The centrally located community of Liptovský Mikuláš, situated between the High and Low Tatras in the Liptov Basin, boasts the

Slovak Republic's liveliest nightlife outside the major cities. Each night, skiers from nearby Jasná flock to the *SkiClub* (ul. 1 Mája 5, Liptovský Mikuláš) bar, whose drinks menu contains over 60 cocktails. The *Route 66 Bar and Restaurant* (Billa Shopping Centrum, Liptovský Mikuláš) offers 'authentic American design' alongside the Slovak Republic's longest bar and a menu of over 150 drinks.

Dining and Cuisine in Slovak Republic

Many Bratislava restaurants are situated within centuries-old buildings, including *Prašná Bašta* (Zámočnícka 11, Bratislava), whose 16th century underground home used to be part of Bratislava's fortifications. Diners can occasionally enjoy live music along with their traditional Slovak cuisine in the restaurant garden. A 19th century Bratislava building houses the *Paparazzi Cocktail Bar and Restaurant* (Laurinská 1, Bratislava), whose most recommended northern Italian dishes are spinach with ricotta and charcoal grilled steaks.

Le Colonial (Hlavná 8, Kosice) serves some of Kosice's tastiest Slovak cuisine inside its intimate interior, while the menu's main courses at *Camelot* (Kovácska 19, Kosice) are all named after the Knights of the Round Table. *Rosto* (Orlia 6, Kosice), Kosice's most popular steakhouse, serves beef from South America and all meats are grilled over an open flame.

Most restaurants in Zilina serve traditional Slovak cuisine, but *Trinity* (Kuzmanyho 100, Zilina) is among the few Asian restaurants in the Slovak Republic's third largest city. *Trattoria Pepe* (J. Vuruma 5, Zilina) is Zilina's most popular Italian restaurant, offering a garden terrace where diners can enjoy pasta and pizza when the weather is warm.

Shopping and Leisure

Bratislava is the Slovak Republic's main shopping hub, boasting several modern shopping malls and designer boutiques which give their counterparts in larger European capitals plenty of run for their money. Sunday is the only day of the week when the shops are closed. Bratislava's biggest shopping malls are Soravia Shopping Palace, Aupark, Avion, Tatracentrum, Danubiana Shopping Center, and Polus City Center. Several Bratislava shopping malls contain banks, photo services, restaurants, sporting facilities, movie theaters, and numerous other non-shopping activities.

Visitors seeking more traditional Slovak souvenirs can find them most easily at the Slovak Republic's six special shops operated by the ULUV, the country's official folk art production center. Elaborately embroidered folk costumes and pillowcases, corn husk and wire crafts, carved wooden figures, and ceramic goods are the most popular handicrafts sold at these shops. Wooden sheep milk pitchers called *črpák*, decorated shepherd's hatchets known as *valaška*, and long wooden shepherd's pipes called *fujara* are also sold in the Slovak Republic's rural sheep farming villages. Bratislava, Banská Bystrici, Bardejov, Košice, Prešov, and Trnava all contain ULUV shops.

Another Slovak Republic shop network called Dielo operates arts and crafts shops in Bratislava, Žilina, Košice, Trenčín, and Banská Bystrica. Most other large Slovak Republic communities also have their own antique shops selling handicrafts by talented local artisans. Borovička juniper berry brandy, Slivovica plum brandy, and wine from at least five different Slovak Republic regions are the country's most popular alcohol offerings. The local Figaro chocolate satisfies any sweet tooth, while *korbáčik* cheese strings, *parenica* steamed cheese curls, *oštiepok* smoked sheep cheese, and *bryndza* processed sheep cheese are sold in all Slovak Republic supermarkets.

Spas

The Slovak Republic's several natural spas and mineral springs have ranked high on the list of the country's most popular attractions ever since 1281, the year of the first written documentation about the territory's healing thermal springs. Today, there are no fewer than 94 destination spas and 1,300 mineral sources in the Slovak Republic.

Most Slovak Republic spas fall into three categories. Balneologic spas treat people with circulatory, digestive, or respiratory diseases, while the climatic spas situated in the mountains mainly treat people with allergies and respiratory issues who benefit from the crisp mountain air. Mixed spas, as their name suggests, are a combination of both. Most spa visitors in the past were wealthy tycoons and royalty. However, today's annual 276,000 spa visitors come from all walks of life, and over 35 percent of them arrive from other countries. Nudity in same-sex bathing facilities is the norm.

In the Slovak Republic, spas are considered a legitimate and affordable form of medical treatment rather than just an expensive privilege for the wealthy. However, that wasn't the case when the 19th century buildings at the country's biggest and best known spa, Piestany, first opened. This scenic retreat just an hour's drive north of Bratislava welcomes over 40,000 patients at its 2,000 beds each year. Piestany's hot mineral springs pack large amounts of mineral substances within their nearly 155°F waters. Piestany even has its own social center offering a plethora of invigorating sporting activities and interesting art exhibits.

Transportation
Slovak Republic Taxis and Car Rental

Slovak Republic taxis are not metered, but they are cheap and readily available. Fares increase after dark. Bratislava visitors should use taxis from *Hello Taxi* (+421 0800 116 321), *Fun Taxi* (+421 02 5477 7377), or any of the capital's 20 other official taxi firms instead of one of the more than 150 independent taxis which have yellow taxi lights on their roofs. Most company-owned taxis, which are safer and cheaper than independent taxis, have their firm's name clearly displayed on the sides of their vehicles.

Visitors can easily obtain and drive rented vehicles throughout the Slovak Republic. Vehicles drive on the right and must always keep their lights on between October 15 and March 15. Emergency telephones are placed about once every half a mile on major Slovak highways, whose quality is generally as good as those elsewhere in Europe. Poorly lit rural roads, winter snow and ice, and speeding traffic are the biggest driving challenges here.

Slovak Republic Water Taxis

Bratislava is the Slovak Republic's major port, and the Danube River is the country's main waterway. Ferry and cruise ship service is available between Bratislava and the cities of Budapest, Vienna, and Hainburg.

Slovak Republic Trains and Buses

InterRail passes allow Rail Europe passengers to travel freely between the Slovak Republic and several other European countries. The Railways of the Slovak Republic lines between Bratislava and most other major Slovak Republic destinations are usually the fastest and cheapest way to travel between cities. Advance reservations are recommended for the busiest routes.

Slovak Lines buses regularly depart Bratislava for destinations across the Slovak Republic, while Eurolines is the main bus line linking the country with the rest of Europe. Bus travel between Bratislava and Prague is usually slower, but cheaper, than rail travel for passengers who make advance ticket purchases. Buses also travel to many places which cannot be reached by train.

Bratislava and other major Slovak Republic cities have their own reliable public transportation network of buses, trams, and trolleys. Slovak Republic inner-city public transportation networks use flat fare systems and allow passengers to use pre-purchased passes. Changing routes usually requires purchasing separate tickets. Bus and tram stops sporting blue badges operate throughout the night. Slovak Republic buses are usually punctual and clean.

Airports

Bratislava Milan Rastislav Štefánik Airport

Just over 1.5 million passengers entered the Slovak Republic's biggest airport in 2011. In addition to the Slovak Republic, this airport's catchment area includes parts of Hungary, Austria, and the Czech Republic. A new Terminal A, doubling the airport's maximum capacity and handling both domestic and international flights, recently replaced the recently demolished original Terminal A. Terminals B and C only handle arriving flights. The building connecting terminals A and B houses a post office and travel agencies.

Budget carrier Ryanair operates a large percentage of this airport's scheduled flights, but other budget airlines available here include Danube Wings, Norwegian Air Shuttle, and UTair. As there are presently no non-stop flights between Bratislava and North America, North American passengers must either first stop at another major European city or fly into the much larger Vienna International Airport and then take ground transportation to Bratislava. Airport amenities include a restaurant with free wireless internet access, a VIP lounge, first-aid facilities, currency exchange, and several shops.

Avis, Budget, Hertz, Europcar, and Sixt stand alongside two local car companies at the airport's car rental section in the Arrivals terminal public area. Public transportation options include taxis, a shuttle service which travels the 5.5 miles between downtown Bratislava and the airport, and city bus 61, which travels between the airport and Bratislava's main rail station. Buses also frequently travel the 34 miles between the airport and Vienna International Airport.

Travel Tips

Language
The Slovak language is similar to that of Czech, spoken in the neighboring Czech Republic, to the point where speakers of both languages can easily understand each other. Hungarian is the first language of nearly 10 percent of the population.

Currency
The euro has been the Slovak Republic's official currency since the country joined the European Union in 2004. Most Slovak Republic ATMs are reliable and most places accept major credit cards. Visa Electron and Maestro are the most commonly accepted debit cards, while Visa, American Express, and Thomas Cook are the most frequently accepted travelers' checks. Slovak Republic banks are closed on weekends. Foreign currency is easily exchanged at major travel agencies, banks, road border crossings, and hotels.

Time

The Slovak Republic shares the same Central European Time Zone, an hour ahead of GMT (GMT +1) as the rest of central Europe. Daylight Savings Time is observed here.

Electricity
Plugs with two round pins and 230 volt electricity at 50 cycles per second are the Slovak Republic's electricity settings, so visitors from places with different settings should bring voltage converters and plug adaptors should they wish to use electrical devices from home here.

Communications
The Slovak Republic's telephone country code is 421. T-Mobile Slovakia, Orange Slovakia, and O2 Telefonica are the country's three cell phone providers, and reception is generally good across the nation. T-Mobile and Orange Slovakia are also among the country's leading internet providers. Virtually all communities have high-speed internet access, and free wireless internet access is available at the Bratislava Milan Rastislav Štefánik Airport restaurant.

Duty-free
Tourists from other European Union nations can purchase alcohol, beauty products, fragrances, and souvenirs at tax-free equivalent prices in the Slovak Republic. European Union visitors can import up to 200 cigars, a kilogram of smoking tobacco, 400 cigarillos, and 800 cigarettes duty-free. Alcohol import limits for European Union visitors

are up to 110 liters of beer, 90 liters of wine, 10 liters of spirits with more than 22 percent alcohol content, and 20 liters of beverages with less than 22 percent alcohol content. Visitors over 17 from non-European Union countries can import up to four liters of wine, a liter of spirits, or two liters of beverages whose alcohol content is less than 22 percent. Visitors over 18 from non-European Union countries may also import up to 200 cigarettes, 50 grams of perfume, 250 milliliters of eau de toilette, and gifts worth up to €175. Visitors may also import unlimited supplies of food, flowers, and medicine for personal use.

Tourist Office
Slovak Tourist Board, Bratislava: +421 48 413 61 46 or http://www.sacr.sk/en/slovak-tourist-board.

Locations

Slovakia is in the geographical center of Europe. It has an area of 49,000 square kilometers. It is surrounded by Ukraine to the east, Czech Republic and Austria to the west, Poland to the north and Hungary to the south. It is home to at least five million people. Slovakia is now becoming a popular destination in Europe because of its rich history and culture.

Bratislava is the capital of this highly-advance country. It is located in southwestern Slovakia. Bratislava is the educational, financial, and political center of Slovakia. It houses the seat of the president and the executive branch of the government as well as the parliament. It serves as a home to well established financial institution and major universities.

Piestany is a unique city in Slovakia. This city attracts tourist who are interested in health and wellness and is well-known for health spas and other therapeutic methods like hot springs and curative mud. Piestany is a nice and affordable retreat for everyone.

Kosice is the second largest city in Slovakia. It is the center of commerce, architecture, science and culture in eastern Slovakia. There are many historic sites that can be seen in this city like the Forgach Palace, St. Elizabeth's Cathedral and St. Michael's Chapel.

Every place in Slovakia offers a piece of Slovakian history and culture. Each region offers a unique way to experience Slovakia, whether be in the food that they serve, the breathtaking attractions and the people; traveling to Slovakia is a one-of-a-kind event.

Regions and things to do

Bratislava

Bratislava region is the smallest region in Slovakia, bordering with Austria and Hungary. It features the capital city - Bratislava, the Little Carpathians and wonderful lowlands of vineyards.

The capital city of this region and of Slovakia is Bratislava. Tourism in Bratislava region offers many historical cultural monuments and folk traditions.

What to visit

Historical View
Take pleasing walks to the historical sightseeings of Bratislava region: Bratislava castle, Devin castle, Michael's Gate, St Martin's cathedral, Primatial Palace, Old City, Slovak National Theatre, Presidential Palace and The Slavin memorial.

The famous museums worth a visit are: Music Museum, Archeological museum, Museum of Transportation, City Museum and Museum of Natural History.

Svaty Jur is a small town in Bratislava region, which is very attractive. Don't miss the Gothic St George's Church.

Marianka is a church complex in the north of Bratislava. It is the oldest pilgrimage place in Slovakia and it used to be famous also in the time of Austria.

Devin Castle

The strategic value of a hill-top fort of Devin at the confluence of two navigable rivers (the Danube and the Morava) will be clear to you at first glance – it is understandable why this was a prized location for about a thousand years. Officially part of the city of Bratislava, Devin is a 15- or 20-minute ride from Old Town by car or city bus (with frequent departures from the Novy Most bus stop). In summer months, river boat connections run to downtown Bratislava and to nearby Hainburg in Austria.

Aquapark

If you would like to swim a little bit, why not drop by Aquapark in Senec. It has toboggans, pleasant atmosphere and you can enjoy the heat of saunas in beautiful wellness center.

Summer Swimming

Water area in Ivanka pri Dunaji is suitable for swimming as well as Velky Drazdiak, Vajnory lake, Zlate piesky and Slnecne lakes near Senec.

Hiking

Devinska kobyla is the most western part of Little Carphathians in Slovakia. It is 400m above the river Morava. The western parts are the most interesting and they are protected from 1964 as a national reservation. Sandberg - the sand terrace is very popular. It dates back to history as a remnant of sea reef and fossils were found there.

Trencin

Trencin region is located in the north-western part of Slovakia. It is the region with famous history mixed with a strong dose of cultural wealth and natural attractions.

Historical Sightseeing

Trencin city belongs to one with the most historical towns in Slovakia. You definitely should not miss the Trencin castle which dates back to the Great Moravia. It also used to be the seat of Matus Cak of Trencin. It was his residential castle in the centre of Matus's land or Terra Mathei. The romantic legend from Turkish times of Omar and Fatima ties to the castle well. Go for a castle tour to hear it, along with other legends. Overall, Trencin castle is really unique and unforgettable for its visitors.

Roman Inscription

It is the most famous epigraphic memory in middle Europe to the north of the river Danube. You can find it on the rock under the castle, saying:

"To the victory of emperors, dedicated by 855 soldiers of II. Legion of an army stationed in Laugaricio. Made to order of Marcus Valerius Maximianus, a legate of the Second Auxiliary legion."

Trencianske Teplice Spa

The spa town Trencianske Teplice belongs to the most beautiful spa towns in Slovakia. All tourists who want to recover, enjoy peace and beauty will find it here. The sulfur water is ideal for treatment of rheumatics, backache, post-operation conditions and problems with musculoskeletal system. Thermal water springs directly in spa pools in the optimal temperature between 36 - 40 °C.

Hammam is the greatest attraction of this town. It is the bath place which comes from 19th century and it used to be the most expensive bath in Trencianske Teplice.

Partizanske observatory

It is a perfect way how to observe the stars above us. The building of observatory is located 1.364km east of Greenwich Meridian. Public and tourists may visit the lecture hall with the latest up-to date audio-visual technique.

Bojnice Castle

Slovakia has dozens of intact castles worth a visit, but Bojnice has probably been restored with more gusto than any of them. Activities for children (but not only for children), a functioning zoo and health spa and extensive grounds make this a lively place to visit. The history of the castle dates back to at least 1113, and in the 19th century the owners made it the seat of a fabulous collection of furnishings and artefacts. Tucked away in the hills above the town.

Banska

Banska Bystrica region is situated in the territory of historical Zvolen region. The largest of all regions is situated in the central part of Slovakia. It borders with Hungary, Nitra region and Trencin region. This place was implemented into Hungarian kingdom in the second half of the 11th century. Turiec, Liptov, Orava and Tekov belonged to this territory, too.

Natural beauties are very significant here - Low Tatras, Slovak paradise, Muranska plain and Little Fatra. Protected natural areas are Stiavnicke mountains, Cerova highland and Polana. They are part of UNESCO biosphere reservation.

Among the caves belong Harmanecka cave with the largest underground space, Bystrianska cave with many bats and Ochtinska aragonite cave.

The Low Tatras

It is a mountain range which is situated between the valleys of the Vah river and Hron river. The highest peaks are Dumbier - 2043m, Chopok - 2024m and Derese - 2004m. Perfect for recreation, walking and hiking. There are numerous hotels, camping sites and ski lifts. You can even meet wild animals like bear, especially in the eastern part of the Low Tatras.

SNP (Slovak National Uprising 1944) Museum
It is the museum in Banska Bystrica which records the influence of Slovak national uprising on the post-war development in Slovakia. It was founded in 1955

Zvolen Castle
This castle is the Slovak national monument. There is an exposition of Slovak national gallery, wooden painted ceiling where you can see the pictures of Roman and Habsburg emperors.

Recreation
Ski resorts in Donovaly and Chopok, spa in Dudince, Kovacova, Sklene Teplice, Sliac and Banska Bystrica belong to the greatest attractions in Banska Bystrica region.

Presov

Presov region is situated in the north-eastern part of Slovakia. It borders with Poland and Ukraine. There are mostly highland and hilly lands. It is the most populous from all eight regions in Slovakia. The most famous towns and cities of this region are Bardejov, Levoca, Kezmarok and Stara Lubovna which were privileged the title a free royal town in the Middle Ages.

Levoca is a town which is situated in the east of the Spis region. It is literally a cultural-historical diamond among Slovak towns. It dates back to 13th century and it was placed on the business road- Via Magna. Rectangular Square is the most attractive together with roman- catholic Church of St Jacob. In 16th century, the main altar was produced in the workshop of Master Paul from Levoca.

Stara Lubovna boasts with the castle which was built at the beginning of 14th century. The most significant event in the history of the castle happened in year 1412 when Treaty of Peace was signed here.

High Tatras
The mountains are situated in the eastern part of Slovakia. Together with its subdivision - High Tatras and Belianske Tatras and Low Tatras, they reach into this region. They border with Poland. In 1949 it was proclaimed the first national park in Slovakia-TANAP- and in the year 1993 they were proclaimed the Biosphere Reservation Tatry by UNESCO. Gerlachovsky peak, Krivan, Rysy, Lomnicky peak, Mengusovska valley, Velka and Mala Studena valley, Strbske pleso,

Skalnate pleso- they all were formed in the tertiary times. Today, they are the most attractive natural gems of High Tatras and Slovakia. The Gerlachovsky peak reaches the highest point in Slovakia - 2654 ASL.

The High Tatras are the highest and most spectacular mountains in Presov region. Thousands of tourists visit this place every year. Either in winter when they come skiing, downhill skiing, cross-country skiing or in the summer to enjoy aquaparks in Poprad or Tatralandia. When you are in Tatras in the summer, you might think wearing shorts and short-sleeved T-shirt is enough to put on hike. But when you find yourself on the snowy mountain, it might not be true. The weather in Tatras is changeable.

Andy Warhol
He was the most famous personality of pop-art. In the town of Medzilaborce, you will find his works of art and artifacts from his childhood and life.

Trnava

Trnava region is located in the southwestern part of Slovakia. Zahorie lowland, Little Carphatians and Danubian lowland form its territory.

It borders with Austria, Hungary, Bratislava region, Trencin region and Czech republic. This territory belongs to the oldest cultural areas of

Slovakia. It has been proved by finding the ancient archeological objects. The most famous is "Moravian Venus". It is more than 22 500 years old. Many nations have lived here: Celts, Germans, Slovenians, Hungarians. They dwelled especially in lowland areas.

The Little Rome!
The center of the Trnava region is the town of Trnava where you can see the cultural and historical attractions. As there are many churches within Trnava's city walls, this town is often called "Little Rome" or "Slovak Rome".

One of the most important churches is the Cathedral of St. John the Baptist. It was the first Baroque church in Slovakia. The wooden altar belongs to the one of the biggest ones in Europe. The Holy Trinity Statue, the statue of St. Joseph, the Ursulinian and Trinitarian Church were constructed later.

The City Tower
If you love the bird view, you certainly should not miss the visit to the City Tower in Trnava. It dates back to renaissance. There are 143 stairs on the way up. You will love this place and it's views.

Piestany
Piestany Spa dominates the Trnava region. It belongs to one of the most famous in Slovakia and people from all around the world visit

this unique town. Thermal springs heal many diseases. The statue of a man – patient breaking his crutch speaks for itself.

Boldog

The oldest inscription of Romans in Slovakia is surprisingly not in Trencin, but in the village of Boldog near Senec. Historians agree that it could be the evidence of the fact that this part of Slovakia might have been a part of Roman Empire.

Water World

If you love water and relax, do not miss the chance to visit Galandia thermal pool in Galanta, Horne Saliby, Dunajska Streda, Velky Meder and Senec.

Nitra

Nitra region and its metropolis - Nitra played an important role in creating the Slovak nation, its culture and its education.

It is one of the warmest and agriculturally most productive centers of Slovak Republic. It borders with Trnava, Trencin and Banska Bystrica region and with Hungary in the south. Zitny Island is the largest river island in Europe between Danube and Small Danube. Tribec, Stiavnice mountains and Pohronsky Inovec are the significant geographical features of Nitra region.

Famous Sites in Nitra Region

Topolcianky Horse-Breeding Farm
This unique place was reconstructed in eighties in the last century. The hippology museum shows you everything what is associated with horses- various breeds of horses, smith, wheelwrights, saddler's workshop, room and kitchen of worker in the stud. Of course, this all is set into historical context.

Nitra Castle
This monument is located on the rocky mountain. It consists of four parts: cathedral, bishop palace, industrial buildings and outer walls of the castle. It dates back to the year 871 AD. The well, historical hill-fort, cathedral and beautiful view through small windows awaits you up there.

Komarno Castle
It is the largest fortress system in Slovakia and also in the whole Austria-Hungary. Its building started in the 16th century and the bridge connects old and new fortress above dike. It is the National cultural monument. Today, it is likely going to be recorded in the world and cultural heritage UNESCO.

Nitra Field Train
It is situated in the Slovak Agricultural Museum in Nitra. Its original track comes from sugar beet railways and its serves only as a tourist

attraction.. There is also a children's little train. So the whole family can enjoy this beautiful site.

Water World in Nitra Region
Podhajska thermal park with ten pools and wellness, Vadas - Sturovo, Spa Patince, thermal pool Santovka wellness and Diakovce are just a few to name the water attractions in Nitra region.

Zilina

Zilina region, the third largest region in Slovakia, is situated in the northern part of Slovakia. It is a varied area and you can find here beautiful valleys, rivers and streams and hills.

The whole area is mountainous and these mountains belong to the Western Carpathians. They include Javorniky, the Greater Fatra, the Lesser Fatra, Oravska Magura, Western, Low Tatras and others.

Must-see in Zilina Region

The Slovak Betlehem
One of the cultural sights you can see there is The largest wooden nativity scene (Slovak Betlehem) in Slovakia. It is located in Rajecka Lesna. It contains more than 170 figures in motion. They were carved from wood and they are exhibited in the house of Gods Nativity. These

are Biblical figures and the copies of the most typical building structures of Slovakia. It is also pilgrimage village.

Oravska Lesna
The historical logging switchback railway in Oravska Lesna is a world historical monument. The similar railway is to be found only in Peru! In the past it used to carry wood. Oravska Lesna is located on the border of Orava, Kysuce and Poland. It is very attractive for tourists because there are ski resorts in this area. It is possible to ski here until April.

Martin
The town Martin houses the oldest and the largest national cultural institution of Slovakia - Matica Slovenska. It is a cultural institution of the Slovaks and it was established in 1863. It was a result of the Slovak national efforts to lay the foundations of Slovak science, libraries and museums.

Other Interesting Places
The following items are the historical, cultural and entertainment sites of Zilina region: Museum of Orava Village - Zuberec, Aquapark Tatralandia in Liptovsky Mikulas, Strecno castle, Demanovska cave of Liberty, Orava Castle, Thermal park Besenova, Meander Park in Oravice, Rafting Ruzomberok, Cutkovo archery in Ruzomberok.

Kosice

Kosice region is the second largest region in Slovakia. It borders with Hungary and Ukraine. The terrain consists of two main land systems - the Eastern Slovak Lowlands and the Spis and Gemer karst.

The largest river in the region is the Bodrog.

Kosice city is the second largest city in Slovakia. You can find there a lot of interesting places. Some of them are: St. Elizabeth Cathedral, St. Urban Tower, St. Michael Chapel, District House, Jakab's Palace and Kosice ZOO. The Main Square in Kosice is one of the most beautiful in Slovakia. It is dominated by the St. Elizabeth Cathedral which was constructed in the fourteenth century. It is proclaimed the national cultural heritage.

Slovak Paradise
Slovak Paradise is one of the nine national parks in Slovakia with 300 kilometers of hiking trails. There are two rivers - Hnilec and Hornad.

Domica cave is located in the Slovak Karst National Park and it is one of the UNESCO national nature monuments. The tour can include a boat ride on the Styx River which flows through the cage.

The Tokaji wine is the world-famous delicious, aromatic wine. It was served at the French Royal court at Versailles. You are cordially invited to taste this wine directly in the wine cellar together with home-made specialties of the Zemplin region.

Krasna Horka Castle
(Castle is closed at the moment because it is being reconstructed due to the extensive fire in March 2012)

The castle of Krasna Horka was constructed in the early 13th century, probably to stand guard over nearby mines, and passed through a number of aristocratic Hungarian families. Then from the 16th century onwards it remained in the hands of the influential Andrassy family, which substantially modified it, first as a successful stronghold against Turkish incursions and later as an impressive manor home. Today it houses an extensive restored museum.

The castle is situated near Roznava, an hour's travel from Kosice or the Slovak Paradise, or two hours from the High Tatras. The best public transport connection is from the town of Roznava (accessible by train from Kosice and the west) by local city bus. Car park directly by castle.

Swimming pools in the Kosice region
The swimming pools Triton, Ryba Anicka and Trebisov swimming pools are there in Kosice region to sooth your body and mind.

Tourist Regions
Liptov
Eastern part of Zilina region

Colorful region, considered the heart of Slovakia by Slovaks. Beautiful mountains and valleys of Low and Western Tatras, ski resorts of Jasna, swimming in Liptovska Mara or priceless cultural monuments. Liptov is simply a paradise!

Demänovská Cave of Liberty

The Demänovská Cave of Liberty is located in the northern part of the Low Tatras in Liptov region within Demänovská Valley. It is the most visited cave in Slovakia.

The path with educational boards in length of 400 m leads to the entrance of the cave in the elevation height 870 m. The duration of the walk is about 10-15 min. Average temperature in the cave is 6,1 - 7°C.

You can choose between traditional and long visit tour. But be careful because the long visit tour is held only once a day.

Traditional Tour

It is 1.150 m long, the camber is 86 m and you climb altogether 913 stairs.

During the visit you can admire unique sinter forms created by underground flow of the river Demänovka, little karst lakes together with rich stalactite and stalagmite decorations and you will be informed about whole history of this remarkable cave.

Long Tour

The long tour has length of 2.150 m and you have to climb 1.118 stairs.

Traditional visit is enriched by "*the Big Dome*" - the biggest underground space accessible for public with underground river bed and soft dead-white sinter, then "*the Pink Hall*"and "*the King's Gallery*", which has the most various decorations in the cave with unique cave water lilies and lake sponge shapes, cave pearls and plenty of other forms of sinter decoration.

Opening hours

Regular ticket price for an adult is 7€ (traditional tour), 14€ (long tour), for children 3,50€ or 7€, students and retired people pay 6€ or 12€. Permission to take pictures costs extra 10€.

The long tour starts at 13:00, in main season at 13:15.

January 2 – February 28 (except Mondays)	from 09:30 until 14:30
March 1 - May 31 (except Mondays)	from 09:30 until 14:00
June 1 – August 31 (except Mondays)	from 09:00 until 16:00

September 1 – November 15 (except Mondays)   from 09:30 until 14:00

December 26 – December 31 (except Monday)   from 09:30 until 14:00

How to get there

By car

The best access by car is from Liptovský Mikuláš through Demänovská Valley direction Jasná.

By bus

from Liptovský Mikuláš, bus stop: "Demänovská dolina, Ľadová Jaskyňa"

Demänovská Ice Cave

The Demänovská Ice Cave is located in the northern part of the Low Tatras in Liptov region within Demänovská Valley. It has the all year long ice filling.

Cave is formed by the underground flow of the river Demänovka. Visit tour leads through spacious river corridors interrupted by steep sections. Its first part takes you to cave spaces with sinter decoration and the second through icy spaces, which is a really impressing combination.

Ice filling is located in the lower parts – it occurs in the form of ground ice, stalactites, stalagmites or ice columns. In cave is a long-known find of bones of various animals, including cave bear, which were once considered as dragon bones - that's why the second name of Demanovska ice cave was *the Dragon's cave*.

The entrance to the cave in reef called "Bašta" can be seen from parking place, but you have to climb up to it for about 20 minutes. The path has resting places and educational panels.

Opening hours of Demanovska Ice Cave

May 15 – May 31 (except Mondays)	from 09:30 until 14:00
June 1 – August 31 (except Mondays)	from 09:00 until 16:00
September 1 – September 30 (except Mondays)	from 09:30 until 14:00
October 1 – May 14	closed

The length of the visit is 650 m and it lasts 45 minutes. Air temperature in the summer months is around 0,4 to 3 °C, so do not forget to take warmer clothes and good shoes. It is advised to relax before the entrance. Relative humidity is 92 - 98 %.

Regular ticket price for an adult is 7€, for children 3,50€, students and retired people pay 6€. Permission to take pictures costs extra 10€.

How to get there

By car

The best access by car is from Liptovský Mikuláš through Demänovská Valley direction Jasná.

By bus

from Liptovský Mikuláš, bus stop: "Demänovská dolina, Ľadová Jaskyňa"

Vlkolínec

If you are in Slovakia for the first time or you are just spending your annual holiday, definitely do not miss the opportunity to visit Vlkolinec - a village in Velka Fatra.

Vlkolinec is the village where historical traditions, houses, habits and craftwork are preserved until today. The number of inhabitants today is not more than twenty. It is a picturesque village because it is one of ten Slovak villages which has been granted a status of a folk architecture reservation - because the village is untouched and has preserved historical monuments from 15th century!

You can see the old houses yourself and dive into the history. Typical house consisted of *pitvor* - the typical corridor in the house, stall, chamber, main room and barns.

The historical atmosphere is revived also by the well in the center of the village. It used to be the only source of drinking water for the inhabitants.

If you want to admire some more historical nature of Vlkolinec, plan a visit in August when Nedela (*Sunday*) is held. Folk carvers exhibit decorative objects, art reliefs and sculptures; you can buy the typical historical objects like *crpak*- a special wooden decorated cup for *zincica*, forms for cheese, kitchen dishes, spoons and pestles.

Hikes and biking in the neighbourhood

In the case you want to train your muscles and are into hiking more than into history, do not omit the hike from Vlkolinec to Malino Brdo - what is a great place for skiing if you visit this area in winter. You can also try the hike from Ruzomberok to Calvary in Vlkolinec.

If you prefer biking, the journey from Ruzomberok - Vlkolinec and back to Ruzomberok might be interesting for you. The length is 12km.

Another option is the biking trip from Ruzomberok - Podsucha - Smrekovica - Ruzomberok. The length of this trip is 32km. Both these trips are for advanced bikers, because they are quite hard. On some places you will even need to get off the bicycles and push it.

Museum of Liptov village in Pribylina

The outdoor museum in Pribylina is an extended exhibition of Liptov Museum in Ruzomberok. It features buildings from the flooded area of Liptovska Mara and some villages of upper and lower Liptov.

The youngest open-air museum in Slovakia is closely connected to the Liptovska Mara dam. Precious buildings, which would have otherwise been flooded, were relocated here to create an unforgettable historical experience for their the visitors.

During a tour we can see the Renaissance chateau with a luxurious interior, mayor's house, municipal school, workshops of a tailor, wheelwright and blacksmith and a firehouse station. The real jewel is an early-gothic Church of Virgin Mary with the original fragments of wall paintings. Identical twin sister of the church's tower stands on the banks of Liptovska Mara.

Pribylina is a very lively place thanks to the many events and seasonal promotions with exhibits of folklore and handicrafts. Children can take a ride on the Hutsul horse (descendants of wild horses in Slovakia) and see the dark Carpathian goats or Wallachian sheep.

Opening hours

Season	Days of operation	Opening hours
1. 1. - 30. 4.	Monday - Sunday	9.00 - 16.00

1. 5. - 30. 6.	Monday - Sunday	9.00 - 17.30
1. 7. - 31. 8.	Monday - Sunday	9.00 - 19.30
1. 9. - 30. 9.	Monday - Sunday	9.00 - 18.00
1. 10. - 31. 10.	Monday - Sunday	9.00 - 17.00
1. 11. - 31. 12.	Monday - Sunday	9.00 - 16.00

Entry fee for adults is 3€; if you want to take pictures, prepare extra 1€.

Prosiecka and Kvacianska valley

Climb through bizarre gorge, wild waterfalls, stunning views of Liptov and a monument of old mills, the walk through picturesque Liptov twins promises all that.

Valleys hidden in deep forests of Choc mountains have a nature of a narrow gorge. Here we find a high cliffs accessible by chains or steel ladders, towers of unusual shapes, high waterfalls and interesting mountain flora and fauna. This landscape-historical delicacy simply must be experienced!

Tourist circuit through Prosiecka and Kvacianska valley takes about 6 hours. The best starting point is the village Prosiek. The route has a length of about 17 km and with a climb to Prosecne (1372 m), from which there's a beautiful view of surroundings, its elevation is around 770 meters. For a less demanding hike, it is possible to omit Prosecne.

Prosiek → mouth of Prosiecka valley → Svorad → Prosecne → Ostruhy saddleback → canyon of Borovianka → Oblazy mills → Kvacany → country lane underneath Choc Mountains to Prosiek

Havránok - Celtic settlement

Open-air museum in Havránok is the most important archeological monument in the Liptov region. It showcases the reconstruction of the Celts farm settlement.

This is an archeological site near Havránok on the top of Úložisko by the reservoir of Liptovská Mara. Patient work of archeologists revealed relics from the Iron (300-100 BC) and the Roman Age. But the highest growth in the region was achieved during the Celtic colonization.

At the present time a reconstruction of part of the Celtic settlement with a sacrifical altar from the 1st century BC is being carried out. Remains of burnt offerings (grain, jewellery) have been found and the bones of seven people, probably victims of religious rituals, were found in a well. From the 11th to the 15th century a wooden Slavonic fort with ramparts stood here.

Being a visitor of Havranok means to touch the oldest history.

Opening hours

May	Mon-Sun from 9:00 to 17:00
June - August	Mon-Sun from 8:30 to 18:30
September - October	Mon-Sun from 9:00 to 17:00

Admission

The entrance fee is only 2€ for an adult. If you want to take pictures, add 0,70€.

Skipark Jasna Nizke Tatry

The largest SKI resort in Slovakia is located in the Low Tatras mountains and offers great conditions for winter sports for expert and beginner skiers. The monument of Jasna is definitely Chopok, the second highest peak of Low Tatras (2024 m), known for excellent ski and hiking options.

Both northern and southern side of Chopok is interconnected, so you can come from Liptovsky Mikulas or Brezno and enjoy it all.

Slopes

The ski resort boasts the longest ski slopes in Slovakia, divided into 5 areas: Záhradky, Jasná, Otupné, Srdiečko and Kosodrevina. There are almost 50 km of slopes, a dozen freeride zones, evening skiing and tracks for kids.

ACTIVITIES

- Fresh Track skiing
- Evening skiing
- Freeride
- Sledging
- Ice-skating
- FUN ZONE
- Snow Park
- Cross-country skiing
- Hurricane Factory
- Nightlife club

How to get to Jasna

Best way to get to Jasna is from the north through the town of Liptovsky Mikulas (located on D1 motorway) and from there through Demanovska dolina (perfect for accommodation and dining as an outpost to Jasna).

From the south it is possible to get to Jasna from the town of Brezno. Direct bus line connects Brezno with Jasna-Srdiecko.

Stanisovska Cave

Janska Valley conceals more than 200 caves, not accessible to the public... except for one. Stanisovska cave opened in 2010 thanks to caving enthusiasts offers a unique atmosphere to be experienced only with the light of your headlamp.

Small Stanisovska cave is located in the northern part of the charming Janska Valley. In an exciting guided tour we discover walls modeled by nature to indescribable and bizarre shapes sometimes covered with cave milk, inscriptions in various languages and mysterious characters from past visitors, small lakes with rare animals, large stalactites, animal bones and shamanic sacrificial place.

Cave tour lasts less than an hour, and its length is about 400 m. Each visitor will receive a headlamp. Good sturdy shoes are recommended.

Opening hours

Open daily with entrance every hour. The first entry at 10.00, last at 16.00 (Saturdays until 19:00). Admission for adults is 6 €.

How to get there

Liptovsky Jan is about 7 km from Liptovsky Mikulas. The cave has a good access, parking is about 200 m far.

Vazecka Cave

In a distinctive village under the Tatras lies a fabulous cave. It is the ancient home of the cave bear, who lived and raised their young there 15,000 years ago.

The cave consists of a long horizontal corridors and halls formed by erosion of the Biely Vah creek. The cave is richly decorated with glistening white stalactites in a wonderful fairy-tale shapes, remarkable lakes with rich sinter decoration of various colors and wall waterfalls. We can find a lot of river sediments here, such as fine gravel or huge cave bear bones.

Length of the tour is 235 m and it takes less than half an hour. It's a quick snack, suitable for small children. A restaurant lies in front of the cave entrance.

Opening hours

Season	Days of operation	Entrance
Spring season (1.2. - 31.5.)	Tuesday - Sunday	9:30, 11:00, 12:30, 14:00

Summer season (1.6. - 31.8.)	Tuesday - Sunday	-	9:00, 10:00, 11:00, 12:00, 13:00, 14:00, 15:00, 16:00
Autumn (1.9. - 30.11.)	Tuesday - Sunday	-	9:30, 11:00, 12:30, 14:00
1.12. - 31.1.	closed		closed

Entry fee for adults is 4 €. Photographing costs extra 7 €.

How to get there

Village of Vazec is located between Liptovsky Mikulas and Poprad. It has good access by car and train. Parking is located directly in front of the cave, on the western edge of the village.

Orava

Orava Castle

One the most beautiful and largest castles in Slovakia, in the northern Orava region, Orava Castle is situated on a high rock above Orava river.

In the forgotten, rough lands of Orava, on the way to Poland, along the Orava river, you will find a rocky formation, a steep rocky cliff vertically erected to the skies. Oravsky Podzamok village (translated lightly as "village under the castle") is the starting point to the mighty Orava Castle.

As it usually goes with Slovak castles, it was built in the place of former fortified fortress. That was right after the Tartar raids, in the mid 13th century. Orava Castle was owned by many aristocrats, county heads and noblemen, protecting important road to Poland and serving as an administrative and military centre for the region.

Nosferatu's Castle

Many of scenes from the famous vampire horror film Nosferatu (1922) were shot in Orava Castle. Other scenes also depict Slovakia's High Tatras and Vah River.

After Francis Thurzo got the castle in pledge in 1556, he reconstructed it extensively, adding supporting walls to statically disturbed parts, annexing a palace and a new chapel. His son continued with works by building a big bastion with a tunnel, gatehouse and gate tower, according to the principals of then modern fortification theories. After his death, to this day, his wife Elizabeth Czobor supervises the castle. At night she walks through castle halls and courtyards with a lantern in her hand.

In 1800 the castle burnt out after several days and nights of fire. Fortunately, Francis Zichy had it repaired and reconstructed almost immediately. Shortly after, one of first museums in Slovakia was established here.

Exhibitions

Journey through the castle will take you hundreds of years aback. Castle buildings, furnished rooms, large courtyards, torture rooms and weapon collections are just a part of one interesting historical exhibition.

Visit of the Orava Castle culminates in the highest and oldest parts - the Citadel. Archeological exposition documents history of the oldest settlements of Orava.

In the middle castle, one can enjoy a natural history exhibitionshowing fauna and flora of Rohace mountains (one of the most breathtaking parts of Western Tatras).

Do not forget to buy an extra ticket to see the magnificent chapel. It is well worth it!

How to get there

- ✓ **By railway** from Kralovany, station Oravsky Podzamok.
- ✓ **By car** from Dolny Kubin towards Poland.

Leave your car on the parking lot in Oravsky Podzamok. You will see immediately how to get to the first castle's gate. The place is very lively.

You cannot photograph inside the castle unless you buy permission for a small extra cost.

Night visit is recommended! (during summer season)

Oravska priehrada (Orava Dam)

The "Orava Sea", spreading on the area of 35 km, has a magical natural scenery, many unique historical places around and even an Island of Art in its middle.

As one of the largest water reservoirs in Slovakia, it is the most visited Orava's tourist destination in the summer.

Orava dam is dotted with resorts (Slanicka osada, Pristav, Stara hora, …), hotels, guesthouses and restaurants.

The dam provides very good conditions for windsurfing, scuba diving, water skiing and yachting. You certainly should not miss a cruise to Slanicky Island of Art, where you'll find a Baroque church full of exhibits of traditional folk art, or you might arrive at the time of a classical music concert.

Sightseeing boat trip by boat SLANICA

May 15 - September 15   9:00 to 16:00

Address: Oravska priehrada - Slanicka Osada: "OG-SLANICA" from the port no. 2

- ✓ estimated shipping according to interest: 9:00, 11:00, 13:00, 15:00, 16:30
- ✓ voyage to the island and back takes about 80 min
- ✓ admission fee for an adult for a whole trip is 4€

SKI Oravice

Modern SKI Oravice resort offers a unique combination of skiing and relax in a thermal park right at the foothill of the slopes. Add a beautiful panoramic views of High Tatras and you get a first-class level of ski experience!

Only 15 km from Polish borders lies a magical ski + thermal park, offering several well-groomed slopes. A fast 4-seater chairlift with heated seats or a ski-lift gets you to 5 wonderful pistes, great for intermediate skier. Three 10 km long cross-country tracks cut across the beautiful surrounding countryside.

A safe kids-park with a small lift and a ski school near the parking lot is available for the little ones. A family ski school teaches skiing and snowboarding on a daily basis.

Drink a hot tea in the buffet directly on the slope. After a good day full of skiing, visit a restaurant which offers a wide selection of local Slovak and Polish dishes.

Spiš

Spis Castle

In the lands of Spis, the north-western region of Eastern Slovakia, large castle is standing proudly on the hill above the plebs.

The Spis Castle was build some 900 years ago, in the 12th century, on the site of an earlier castle. As an important political, economic and cultural center for this part of Kingdom of Hungary, several kings and families owned the castle. Now, a property of state of Slovakia, 'Spissky Hrad' (in Slovak), one of the largest castles in Europe, is living vividly as a tourist's favorite spot.

History

Surrounding stone fortification protected the inner Romanesque palace from the Tartars while raiding our lands in 1241. In the half of 15th century, king donated the castle to the noble Zapolsky family.

They rebuilt the Romanesque palace into Gothic style, they thickened and elongated the tower and overall they took good care of the castle. Even if the family owned 70+ castles, Spissky Hrad was their preferred seat. Ján Zápoľský, the last king before Habsburgs, was born at the castle

Habsburgs gave the castle to Turzo family and they then rebuilt it in the Renaissance style. The last family that owned the castle (till 1945!), the Csákys, left it in ruins after the fire in 1780. After war, the castle underwent repairing, reconstructing and archeological research. Now, it serves as a museum and exposition piece at the same time.

Spis Castle Today

Several movies like Dragonheart or The Last Legion were filmed here. No wonder, you can almost feel the history talking to you.

In the archeological part of the exhibit you can see findings from the Stone Age until the Middle Ages. Roman coins were also find inside narrow dark cave under the castle. Castle's kitchen is nicely restored, you can almost see the cooks preparing food for castle's lords. Over-the-top feasts were sometimes held for almost 4 hours. Castle's bedroom, washroom, armory, chapel and torture room are also interesting parts of the exposition. Be sure to climb up the tower! You will be treated to an excellent view perfect for photographing.

Opening Hours

The Spis Castle is closed during winter.

Season starts in April. The castle is open daily 9:00 - 18:00 (October - April: 9:00 - 16:00).

Admission fee for an adult is 5€.

Around the Castle

There are other beautiful locations worth a visit in this area. Spisska Kapitula, often called 'Vatican of Slovakia', is a part of Spisske Podhradie, province under the castle. Gothic architecture, Baroque decorations on houses, Romanesque churches, cathedral and on top of that, beautiful view on High Tatras. The Church of the Holy Spirit in Zehra, one of the earliest Slovak settlements, showcases high quality wall paintings from the Middle-Ages. The complex is on UNESCO's World Heritage List among 1.000 of the most important monuments in the world.

Dobšinská Ice Cave

One of the most famous ice caves in the world and the largest ice cave in Slovakia. The ice filling has a volume of 110.132 m3 and occurs in the form of ground ice, waterfalls, ice stalagmites and columns.

Dobsinska Ice Cave has several magnificent parts – halls, corridosr and domes. Thanks to the icy air, which lies down deep, the cave is full of fantastic ice formations and glaciers that sometimes fill it up to the ceiling. The thickness of the ice filling in the Great Hall is as much as 26.5 metres!

The 1 km long ascent route to the cave's entrance is lined with educational boards and takes about 25 min. Duration of the visit is half an hour and 515 m. Air temperature drops to -3°C, make sure to wear good warm clothes.

Regular ticket price for an adult is 7€. Permission to take pictures costs extra 10€.

The cave is open May 15 - Sept 30 (except Mondays), every hour until 16:00.

How to get there
Access by car is from Poprad through Vernár (direction Rožňava).

By bus:

Ski Mlynky
SKI MLYNKY - holiday in the heart of the Slovak Paradise. SKI MLYNKY invites you to great skiing on its slopes and for the lovers of cross-country skiing there are kilometers of cross-country trails available.

Welcome in the most important ski resort in the Slovak Paradise - Ski Mlynky. It consists of three ski resorts - Gugeľ, Dedinky and Biele vody.

Ski Mlynky complex offers many opportunities for winter sports - 9 ski trails, 7 lifts and 35 km of cross-country trails. Visitors have range of services to their disposal, from rental of ski equipment to catering services and accommodation in the area.

The ski resort is situated on the nearby hills with an elevation of 92 m to 210 m.

Ski resorts of Ski Mlynky

GUGEL

Northern slopes of the hill Gugel. The centre is equipped with three lifts, 7 slopes.

Trails

- ✓ Gugel-Tourist 1400 m
- ✓ Gugel-Tourist / solar 400 m
- ✓ Gugel-Chimney 1000 m
- ✓ Gugel-Winter well 700 m
- ✓ Gugel-Summer well 900 m
- ✓ Gugel-Wheel free ride 700 m
- ✓ Gugel-Baby 150 m

The resort offers two cafeterias. The first buffet awaits you at the lift platform and the second bar will refresh you on a sunny slope. Parking spaces are located near the lift. Distance to Biele vody skipark is about 1.5 km, Dedinky about 5 km.

BIELE VODY

Northeastern slopes of Hajik hill.

Trails

- ✓ Small 200 m
- ✓ Large 550 m

Parking lot is located right next to the lift, bar and ski rental. Distance to center Gugel is about 1.5 km and 4.5 km to Dedinky.

DEDINKY

Ski resort uses northwestern slopes of the Hajik hill. It is equipped with two lifts and two ski runs and the third slope for other winter activities. Distance to Biele vody is about 4.5 km and Gugel about 5 km.

Trails

- ✓ Bambini 80 m
- ✓ Large 520 m
- ✓ Bobsleigh 600 m

Parking is under the Priehrada hotel.

visas
Visa application requirements for Slovakia

Slovakia is part of Schengen, an area in the European Union where people may travel freely without having to undergo border checks from the various countries that make up this group. Member states that make up the Schengen area are Austria, Belgium, Czech Republic, Denmark, Estonia, Finland, France, Germany, Greece, Hungary, Iceland, Italy, Latvia, Lithuania, Luxembourg, Malta, Netherlands, Norway, Poland, Portugal, Spain, Slovakia, Slovenia, Sweden and the Swiss confederation. They also adopt a uniform visa policy.

Many countries have an agreement with the Slovak Republic that doesn't require its citizens to apply for a visa to enter the country. To see if one is covered by the visa exemption you may contact their nearest embassy in your locale to find out.

For those who need to apply for a visa, you must present or accomplished the following requirements:

- A passport that is valid for at least up to six months - A fully completed and signed application form - A recent colored I.D. picture - The purpose of the trip - Proof of funds either in the form of a bank statement or traveler's checks that will be use during the travel and stay in the country or the Schengen area. - An onward or return ticket or a confirm itinerary. - Valid travel and insurance documents with a minimum amount of at least thirty thousand Euros. - Proof of visa fee payment.

These requirements may vary or change depending on the purpose of the visit and stay and the Slovak republic may change its visa policies from time to time.

Health and Safety

Ticks carrying Lyme disease are the biggest health risk visitors will encounter, especially those who spend a lot of time hiking in the country's large parks and rural forests. Avoiding thick undergrowth and tall grass is the best way to escape these ticks, but those who spot them on their bodies should immediately and gently remove them with latex gloves and tweezers. The Slovak Republic's tap water ranks among the world's cleanest and food hygiene standards are on par with the rest of Europe. Visitors with valid European Health Insurance Cards may receive emergency health care at no or reduced cost during their stay in the Slovak Republic. Pharmacies are the only places visitors can purchase over-the-counter drugs here.

The Slovak Republic is far safer than it is portrayed in the 2006 film Hostel. Real-life tourists stand virtually no chance of experiencing any type of violent crime, let alone kidnapping, during their stay in one of Europe's safest countries. Poorly-lit roads along with pickpockets in rail and bus stations are the biggest dangers visitors will encounter. Although wolves and bears still roam the Slovak Republic's wilderness, tourists rarely encounter them and nobody has been killed by a bear here for over 100 years.

Climate
The Weather and Climate in Slovakia

Slovakia, generally, have what they call a continental climate. The country has four different seasons but because the country has a mountainous region, the Carpathian Mountains which spans to half of the country, temperatures may differ greatly in different parts of the country.

During winters, temperatures averages at the 9° to 10° C range and have recorded a low of -3° in the lowland region, where the capital, Bratislava is located; while the highland region would tend to hover at around -5° C, but on some rare instances, temperature can go as low as -20° C. During summer, thermometers would register at around 19° C in the lowlands and the highlands would have a hot weather at

15° C. So basically, the country have a mild winter climate except on the mountain tops but most times of the year, except during the summer season, skiers and snowboarders would have a field day of fun in the snow. Thanks to a friendly winter that covers Slovakian slopes around 130 days of the year, Slovakia is, truly, fast becoming a skiing haven among Germans, Poles and Czechs, the usual visitors. In fact, in 2006, total number of skiing tourists has already reached 1.6 million.

Rainfall in Slovakia averages 650 mm of precipitation. Usually, heavy downpour do not cause landslides or avalanches, but they do cause damage to properties located near the rivers Danube, Hron and Vah as a result of an overflow.

Slovakians are spared from nature's wraths like hurricanes and tornadoes as the Carpathian and the Tatras shields them from such weather calamities. However, Slovakians do experience fierce winds but usually a speed of 70 kph is, at the least, an alert of level 1 to other countries.

Best Time to Visit Slovak Republic
Each of the Slovak Republic's four seasons lasts three months and comes with its own unique treasures. The warmest months, from May to September, are the country's busiest tourism months, but the

coldest winter months, from December to April, are the Slovak Republic's prime skiing months.

The early spring months of March and April, along with the fall months from October to the middle of November, are the Slovak Republic's low tourism seasons, but visitors who don't mind the unpredictable weather these seasons bring can stumble upon some spectacular bargains and virtually deserted attractions. The earlier fall months of September and October can also be dry, sunny, and pleasant. Hotels should be booked a year in advance during New Year's Eve, state holidays, and major festivals.

www.ingramcontent.com/pod-product-compliance
Lightning Source LLC
Chambersburg PA
CBHW021107080526
44587CB00010B/417